SURVIVE AND CONQUER

SURVIVE AND CONQUER

TEXAS IN THE '80s:
Power—Money—Tragedy. . . Hope!

M. Ray Perryman

TAYLOR PUBLISHING COMPANY
Dallas, Texas

Published by Taylor Publishing Company
1550 West Mockingbird Lane
Dallas, Texas 75235

Library of Congress Cataloging-in-Publication Data

Perryman, M. Ray (Marlin Ray). 1952–
Survive and conquer : Texas in the '80s : power—money—tragedy—hope! / M. Ray Perryman.
p. cm.
ISBN 0-87833-739-3 : $17.95
1. Texas—Economic conditions. 2. Texas—Economic policy. 3. Business cycles—Texas. I. Title.
HC107.T4P465 1990
330.9764′063—dc20 90-11317
CIP

Printed in the United States of America

10 9 8 7 6 5 4 3 2 1

DEDICATION

To my girls, Skye Lynn and Bethany Rae,
who survived the 1980s with me on the road.

CONTENTS

ACKNOWLEDGMENTS

More people than I can begin to count played a vital role in making this book a reality. When a person as busy as I am tackles a project of this magnitude, it takes an army of support to pull it off. I can't begin to call everybody by name.

A whole group of research assistants from Perryman Consultants, Inc., diligently compiled a data base of information according to my specs. That task wasn't easy. John-Mark Spradlin and Ginnie Johnston coordinated much of this effort, and Jennifer Richter entered it into our software system. Ginnie, John-Mark, Donna Humphrey, Dennis Jeter, and Kevin Gleghorn provided additional research support throughout the process. Shelia Smith, (our data base manager), Dr. Frank Wyman (our statistical research director), and Bob Orvis (our systems analyst and President of Perryman Data Services, Inc.) kept a steady stream of numbers flowing my way.

Jan Rowell supervised the entire manuscript preparation process, assisted by Jennifer, Eliska Smith, Stacey Aucoin, Angelica Cavazos, and Karen Smith. I was also aided by three professional editors at various points in the process—Nancy Cunningham, Avery Hunt, and my old friend Bill Bancroft. Arnie Hanson and his colleagues at Taylor Publishing Company were invaluable in the final phases of manuscript preparation. Lisa Stinson, Dennis Hill, and Patrick Pollei did an excellent job in preparing the jacket. My friend, Ann Christian, also offered a lot of helpful suggestions.

I owe a special debt of gratitude to Jim Moncrief, who traveled a lot of miles with me and brought many ideas to the table. Dr. Larry Lyon, the Director of the Center for Community Research at Baylor University, also logged a lot of miles across the state. I am forever grateful to my many friends who encouraged me to continue this effort in the midst of my other responsibilities. Skipper Dippel, Glenn Biggs, Jere Ruff, and L. E. Sheppard come immediately to mind, but there were many others.

Baylor University and the Brown Foundation have supported my research over the years. I wouldn't be in a position to write this book if it had not been for the scores of student workers and professional associates that have passed through our organization. The voluntary support of my wife, Nancy, during those early years was essential to things moving forward. She was there before I had staff, budget, computers, data, or anything else. My schedule is a strain on my family, and I appreciate their support.

Leigh Martinez, my partner in Perryman Consultants, Inc., has lived through part of the 1970s and all of the 1980s in the activities that I talk about in these pages. She has been there when I needed her. She also did some tough prodding, editing, and organizing to get this one done. Carol Wilhite, my lifelong friend and Executive Assistant, helped with editing, ideas, coordinating, and scheduling. Her own survival of the 1980s was a source of inspiration and encouragement.

My final debt is to the people of Texas. This is their story, and I'm honored to be the scribe. I've made thousands of friends all over the state in the 1980s, and many of them made it possible for me to be on the scene. My fellow Texans are a great bunch of folks, and I hope I do them justice.

PREFACE

Survive and Conquer is a book about one of the most overwhelming periods in the history of any region of this country or even the world. For a lot of folks, the 1980s in Texas seem complex. There were certainly enough things going on a fill a few libraries. When you really get down and look at it, though, the entire decade can be explained by resorting to one simple rule. I've been talking and writing about it for a long time now, so much so that people often refer to it as Ray's Law of Economics. The essential premise from which all economic behavior ultimately springs and all noble truths can be uncovered is that *the most important thing is what people think.*

While I may be the first to say it quite so bluntly and without a bunch of mathematical symbols attached to it, the idea that expectations drive consumer and business decisions has been around for centuries. We spend, save, build, drill, invest, work, and do just about everything else because of what we think is going to happen. If more people would learn this basic fact, the whole "Dismal Science" of economics might become at least tolerable. Being a patriotic Texan, I confess that I may have a strong tendency to lace this tale with maudlin sympathy. I will make every effort to avoid that temptation and will hopefully be successful in most cases. If I'm known for anything, I'm known for "calling 'em like I see 'em." The story of Texas in the 1980s cannot be jaded with superlatives. We can't pretend that there was no pain. Too many people, thousands and thousands of them, were hurt too much. Fortunes were lost, careers sacrificed, communities permanently altered; the daily struggle for existence at times took on epic proportions. The 1990s have begun, and they offer considerable promise. I'm the guy who said we were going down in the 1980s, yet I feel a great deal of optimism about the future. But the story of the 1980s must be clearly told and fully understood if the next decade is to fulfill its potential. I'll give it my best shot.

ONE

A Sigh of Relief

I was tired, but couldn't sleep. It was 2:30 in the morning on January 1, 1990. I had just returned from a New Year's Eve party that has become a tradition for me. This small gathering of a few close friends is a rare indulgence in a schedule that permits little time for socializing. I really needed the break, and, like Merle Haggard's song, "I had a beautiful time." Besides, the hostess is a great cook, a trait that I find particularly endearing.

Like most years, I was a little late getting to the party. Although I'm embarrassed to admit it, I was working right up to the last minute. In fact, I had a full day planned for New Year's Day as well. Things were happening. Big things. Things that could alter the course of history. As a 5′7″ kid from the thriving metropolis of Lindale, Texas, I was thrilled to be in the middle of it all. I wasn't at all sure how I got here, but I was willing to work as hard as necessary to do my part.

Why couldn't I get to sleep? Why was I so uncharacteristically edgy and nervous? I was tired from a long and intense day, and the party had been very relaxing. I should have nodded off immediately, but I didn't. I felt major forces pulling me in many directions at the same time. Suddenly, the source of my conflicting emotions dawned on me. It was simply the fact that it was, indeed, January 1, 1990. My home state of Texas, after much wailing and gnashing of teeth, had survived the 1980s.

My thoughts raced back and forth across the people, places, and events that were a part of this most chaotic decade. Texas has never seen anything like it; we hope to Davy Crockett that we never do again. As I reflected on my own experiences over the past ten years, I could sense the historic and unprecedented nature of this time and place. I could almost feel everybody in the entire state, about 17 million of us, breathing a huge collective sigh of relief.

As I lay in bed staring out into the darkness, images kept bombarding my consciousness, coming in and out of focus—images not of what would happen in the years ahead, but of what had happened in the decade just finished. It was as though I had plugged a videotape of "Texas in the 1980s" into my mind and was fiddling around with the remote control, randomly rewinding and fast forwarding, rummaging through first one event and then another.

I felt fear, happiness, concern—a whole range of emotions. I was, after all, one of the actors in many of the scenes. Like most other folks, though, the biggest thing I felt was relief. After a harrowing ten years, Texas, it was clear, had made it through an unprecedented period in its history. This New Year's Day was not quite the celebration of success that many Texans had anticipated it would be a few years earlier. Nonetheless, we had plenty of reasons to be party animals. Not only had we endured, but the bad times had in some ways tempered us; we had begun to build a solid foundation for a bright and prosperous future. The mere fact that the year ahead didn't have an "8" in it was in and of itself a fine excuse for a rousing get-together.

It's funny the way the mind works (especially mine). For me, at least on that sleepless early morning, it raced around from event to event in no particular order, making no particular point. The good was mixed with the bad, often obscuring meanings. I had to work at figuring out what I was seeing. It was all jumbled up in my head. And maybe that was the way it should be, for the good was mixed with the bad so much during the '80s; the final outcome wasn't always obvious. It definitely wasn't over 'til it was over. This time, the fat lady sang "Auld Lang Syne."

My mental newsreel started on another New Year's Eve, the one just before 1986. That year marked the 150th birthday of the creation of the poor, fledgling Republic of Texas following the Battle of San Jacinto. The Sesquicentennial celebration was to have been an all-out, rip-roaring extravaganza. The party had seemingly been in the works forever. When we started the planning process several years earlier, the state and most of its cities were flush with money from the oil and construction booms. The great bash itself started with a fantastic display of fireworks over the Dallas skies.

Ironically, just as the yearlong fiesta was getting cranked up, oil prices plummeted. The state fell into its second severe downturn in what would prove to be a most trying and difficult decade. It put a real damper on what was supposed to be the party to end all parties.

By the time Britain's Prince Charles arrived in San Antonio a few months later to cut the Sesquicentennial birthday cake in the shadow of the hallowed Alamo, it was clear that the arrival of middle age for the state didn't necessarily signal that maturity had been achieved (the same has been said of me). Texans were learning that, despite our incessant bragging, we were really little more than participants in an economy driven very much by nature's bounty. We had not yet reached the stages of development represented by true diversification, but we were making progress.

The images persisted. In a blur of mental flashes backward and forward, I was beginning to get some sense of the old Texas and the new Texas somehow needing to come to grips with each other in the midst of a complex and ever changing global environment. It was like they were changing the rules on us. My videotape settled on a conversation that I had a few years back with Alan "Bud" Shivers, Jr. about his father. The occasion was a memorial conference at the University of Texas in honor of the late Governor Shivers. Just before I went out to take my place on the platform, Bud shared with me the fact that, shortly before his death, the Governor (I could never call him anything else) had purchased a personal computer. He was just trying to keep up with the times. The notion of our former independent and flamboyant chief executive, by then in his late seventies, sitting down in front of a tube, typing in commands and trying to harness the power of this strange new machine, somehow symbolized to me a merger of the past, present, and future of Texas.

As I continued to try to shut down my brain for a bit of rest, my thoughts turned to another set of contrasts. This time the subject was my many friends from the oil patch. At the beginning of the 1980s, wildcatters, those legendary Texans who put it all on the line to put holes in the ground, were rolling in money and confidence. It didn't seem to matter how many deals they put together or even that the terms of those deals gave them increasingly higher returns; they couldn't get new ones done fast enough to satisfy a clamoring investor market. Doctors, housewives, and just anybody else who could scrape together $10,000 or so were lining up to buy part of an oil well. A few years later, one of the most often told dumb jokes about the sad state of affairs in Texas involved a bank that was giving away oil wells when you opened a new account. Disgruntled customers would ask, "Don't you have any toasters?"

Bankers fueled the frenzy. Oil prices were going to jump to $85 a barrel by 1985, they thought, and they would finance the expanding exploration business and make a killing for themselves along the way. They called the wildcatters on the telephone and went to see them in person, offering big loans collateralized by the very rigs those dollars would build. The wildcatters took the money, leveraging themselves to the hilt in the process.

Then, in 1986, the Saudi Arabian royal family decided to break the backs of the cheating countries who were fellow members of the Organization of Petroleum Exporting Countries (OPEC). They let oil prices plummet from the high twenties down into the teens and even as low as $9 a barrel. Many of the wildcatters who had weathered a downturn by the skin of their teeth in 1982 were totally wiped out, victims of a private decision made halfway around the world.

In essence, they were simply swept away in the wake of a global power struggle; they were scarcely even minor players, or, for that matter, informed spectators. With the wildcatters went all but the strongest in the oil service business, too. Eddie Chiles, whose Western Company of North America was once so flush with cash that it could afford to buy hours and hours of air time for Eddie's famous "I'm mad" commercials, saw his vast drilling empire declare bankruptcy. Lone Star Steel, which made drilling pipe at its plant in East Texas, extinguished most of the fires in its furnaces and laid off thousands. Rigs, pipe, mud, bits—it didn't matter what the businesses made or sold or serviced. The downturn in oil prices shattered their world and sent many to the modern counterpart of debtors' prison.

By the end of the '80s, scores of plants and depots from one corner of the state to the other were like abandoned ghost towns. Once vibrant communities in East Texas, West Texas, and South Texas were seeing a way of life vanish into thin air. Buildings were boarded up, while the expensive machinery inside was gathering dust. Outside, remnants of oil derricks and huge stacks of steel pipe rusted. The lesson was a tough one, but it had to be learned. Texans could no longer count on oil to fuel their economy.

From the oil patch, my thoughts raced to real estate, another sore spot of contrasts in the '80s. The first pictures in this sequence were of forests of construction cranes (known affectionately as the State Tree of Texas) gracing the skylines of major cities, of glum-looking roughnecks living in hurriedly acquired house trailers in Odessa, and of whole square miles in North Dallas being under construction all at once.

Oil had boomed in the 1970s, creating jobs which in turn generated the demand for offices, houses, warehouses, and shops. When the '80s began, though, there wasn't enough space in which to live or work. That demand, along with changes in tax and banking laws, led to more building activity than we had ever imagined, much less seen.

Banks, savings and loans, insurance companies, and other investors had more money to lend than they had places to lend it. Texas, with its seemingly unquenchable thirst for new structures, looked like the best place to put it. With oil a less attractive industry to finance, some of the folks behind the big desks thought real estate could pick up the slack and keep earnings soaring with the seagulls.

Along the way, though, the bottom fell out of the real estate market. Out-of-work roughnecks left the state to find new opportunities elsewhere. Economies in Michigan and other "Rust Belt" states began to inch forward and workers stayed home to take jobs rather than migrating to Texas. Corporate relocations didn't come as fast. New stores didn't spring up as rapidly. Office project owners started begging for renters, giving away free rent and other amazing amenities.

Eventually, bankers began repossessing these buildings. And then the banks and savings and loans themselves began to fail, overburdened by gushers of bad real estate loans. Other Real Estate

Owned (OREO), a nice way of saying repossessed property, became a larger and larger part of portfolios. By the end of the decade, while driving through downtown Dallas showing the sights to an out-of-state client as though I were a tour guide, I remember pointing to one big bank building after another. Like gigantic tombstones, they marked the sites of defunct banks, such as MCorp, InterFirst, and Republic. Not long ago, these institutions were among the state's largest and the nation's most profitable.

My thoughts also turned to people . . . all types of people from all walks of life. One of my friends has conservatively estimated that I talked with at least half a million folks during the 1980s. They started flashing rapidly before me. I visited with the rich and powerful and, all too often, the once rich and powerful. In the course of my work, I spend a great deal of time with those who labor in economic development and social agencies. I saw them struggling to meet human needs and to resuscitate ailing economies. I talked a great deal with people who were simply trying to make a living. Individuals who once held rewarding jobs in the oil or construction industries found themselves lacking a sense of direction. They just wanted a job, any job. Hundreds of thousands of high-paying positions disappeared from Texas at various points in the decade. The families who depended on oil and gas royalties for their well-being suffered mightily. The bright young graduates who rushed into promising careers in banking and finance suddenly found themselves pounding the pavement, looking for work in a glutted market. The psychological toll on self-esteem was incomprehensible, and families lived in the fear and stress created by an uncertain economic future.

These were not casualties of some faraway tragedy. These were friends, former students, and even my neighbors across the street. The economic downturn hit all of us right where we lived.

Next, my mind recoiled to major events, both positive and negative, that shaped the fortunes of Texas in the 1980s. The oil glut. The numerous, failed attempts of a group of oil producing countries to act in their collective best interest. The slashing of North Sea prices. The war between Iran and Iraq. The demise of Global Marine and the first round of Texas bank failures. On the political front, there were federal and state tax laws, streams of financial legislation, and perpetual attempts on the part of Texans to raise the issue of oil import fees to an almost religious plane.

But as the newsreel played on, I saw how vivid impressions of the bust in oil and gas, real estate, and banking obscured a lot of the good times. Indeed, there were some memorable moments. I recalled when retired Admiral Bobby Ray Inman walked into our lives to head Austin-based Microelectronics and Computer Technology Corporation (MCC), the consortium formed to beat the Japanese in discovering the secrets of artificial intelligence and building the next generation of computers.

What a compliment it was that MCC picked Texas. It validated our sense that Texas had the environment, the brainpower, and the training facilities to go head to head with any other place in the expanding intelligence-based economy. Austin was as good a place for a super research and development company as Palo Alto, Boston, or Chapel Hill. Our universities, particularly the engineering schools at the University of Texas at Austin and Texas A&M, measured up well against the programs in the Ivy League and on the West Coast.

In what was another of so many ironies of the decade, Austin real estate developers misinterpreted the MCC signal. Texans do tend to let things go to their heads. They (and a few of their friends from other places) used it to justify an unparalleled burst of building activity that ended abruptly when most of those impressive edifices could not be rented or sold. It was as if they were building for 300,000 new jobs, rather than the 300 or so that MCC would generate.

The Superconducting Super Collider came next into my vision. Waxahachie won an intense national competition for the multibillion-dollar atom smasher, to be built under the green pastures and rolling hills of Ellis County. Scientists from around the world would be coming to the Dallas area to do their research on the largest machine of its type ever to be constructed.

Sematech, another research consortium dealing with research on computer chips, also chose Austin to set up shop. Meanwhile, slowly but surely, the aerospace industry, fueled by billions of federal dollars, had been expanding in North Texas. LTV, Bell Helicopter, and General Dynamics served as its nucleus, but more than 200 local companies were in on the action. Clearly, the state benefited from Ronald Reagan's "Star Wars" defense policies and Majority Leader (and later House Speaker) Jim Wright's political clout.

Mexico, too, turned out to be a source of extraordinary contrasts. Good news and bad news. In the early '80s, when our neighbor to the South was living high on the hog with its overvalued currency, Mexican citizens poured money into Texas. They bought homes on South Padre Island and invested in businesses as far north as Houston and San Antonio. They flooded our banks with funds, seeking a safe haven for their newly found wealth.

Then, the bottom fell out in Mexico, too, with a plunge in the value of the peso that left destitute even relatively well-off people. By the middle of the decade, Mexico began to change, ultimately embracing the concept of a free market economy.

The maquiladoras, several hundred of them strung along the Texas-Mexico border from Brownsville to El Paso, were the harbingers of that change. Big companies like General Motors, Zenith, and Motorola built more and more of these factories, shipping raw materials and components across the border to Matamoros, Juarez, Reynosa, and Nueva Lardeo where they were assembled into final products with cheap labor. These goods were then shipped back to the U.S. for sale and worldwide distribution.

The maquilas needed workers and the workers spent money on the U.S. side. Texas suppliers found good markets in the maquilas, and they expanded. Ultimately, as the decade came to a close, the border cities became so vigorous that even a severe freeze in 1989 which killed the citrus and vegetable crops had only a minimal effect on their overall economic numbers.

The monumental forces and larger-than-life events of the 1980s set a pattern for the 1990s. The newsreel was now moving on to these as yet unfinished stories. The Pennzoil-Texaco affair focused attention on the fundamental issues of reform in the civil justice system which would be confronted in the 1990s. A court ruling agreed with the contention of a small district that our way of getting money to elementary and secondary schools in Texas was unfair to poor areas. This decision, coupled with a need for radical changes in our educational delivery system, insured that the '90s would be an era to address this all-important issue on a grand scale. After more false starts than anyone could count and the removal of virtually all Texas ownership from our major financial institutions, Congress gave us the Resolution Trust Corporation (RTC) as a potential means of coping with our excessive real estate and sick banks and thrifts. With Fort Worth Alliance

Airport seeing its first activity, the 1990s promised to be a period of far-reaching business development.

As my mental videotape finally wound to an end, I was left with some rather obvious truths. The big, swaggering State of Texas has always been a place of enormity. Natives like myself have for years told jokes about how things were bigger in Texas, better in Texas; we treat our native soil with a sense of reverence. Much of that feeling may well stem from the fact that Texas was once an independent nation. We learn from the time that we are in diapers that to live in Texas is to be among the chosen. Whatever the reason, the 1980s taught us that Texas could indeed be as vulnerable as it once seemed invincible. The bigness never went away, as the issues and events shaping the fortunes of the state, both good and bad, were of gargantuan proportions. Even when we went down, we went down in a big way. We called it "the worst boom we had seen in a long time." The '80s further demonstrated that, as much as we might hate to admit it, all things Texan are not always by definition the best. Excruciating hardships were suffered, major crises were endured, and many of the losses can never be recouped. The legacy of generations evaporated in the blinking of an eye. Effects of the tragedies still linger, and they will continue to be with us for quite some time.

Yet Texas endured. Not only that, it became stronger. You are supposed to learn from your mistakes, and those of us in Texas learned that we couldn't live on our natural resources alone. We couldn't live by simply bragging and waiting for the telephone to ring. We couldn't live by leveraging ourselves up to our eyeballs on every front.

The future, we learned, was education. It was diversity. It was a people-based economy. It was a global approach. It was selling ourselves. It was prudently using our capital.

New Year's Day in 1990 clearly did not bring us any radical changes. In fact, this day was, in most ways, very much like the one before it. The new decade did, however, bring an important symbolic opportunity to leave the past behind and press onward in a positive manner. Believe me, we needed one of those.

As I look back on the 1980s, it is difficult to believe that I was a part of so many of these events. I often ponder the simple question of "Why me?" When the decade began, I was a green professor at a private university, tinkering with an untested economic model of the state and trying to build a halfway decent reputation as a thinker. At the close of the decade, I found myself surrounded by a remarkable team of dozens of highly-skilled and dedicated professionals that maintain one of the largest sets of models and economic information in the world. It seemed that, by merely answering the telephone, I had been thrust into major economic development initiatives, task forces addressing a variety of issues, landmark litigation and legislation, the oil and banking/real estate crises, and virtually all of the major new announcements that occurred within the state.

There are probably a fair number of reasons for my involvement. I would like to say that I planned it, but nothing could be further from the truth. The only thing I ever plan is lunch, although I do take that task very seriously. Obviously, my educational background had something to do with it. You don't just wake up one day and decide to build economic models. Timing made a difference as well. I happened to emerge as the guy with all the numbers at the same time that everybody decided that things were changing and they wanted to see more numbers.

My capacity for hard work also came in there somewhere. I generally end up working at least sixteen and sometimes even twenty-four hours a day; whatever it takes to get the job done. I think the fact that I'm a native Texan had something to do with it. I grew up believing in the greatness of Texas and refused to surrender that premise no matter what the odds. It also came out of my days as a kid in East Texas feeling that I could tackle just about any project that needed to be tackled. Whenever anybody asked if we would do something, we said "Yes!" Before long, a lot of folks were calling. As it became more and more apparent that Texas was having serious problems, my old nationalistic juices started flowing. I would do whatever it took to help Texas, and everybody knew it. I wish I could give a better explanation, but that's the best I can do.

I traveled a million miles and saw the acts and scenes where the miraculous play that was "Texas in the 1980s" was performed. I frequently ventured into the big cities, the rural areas, the oil patch, and relatively obscure places where the winds of change were blowing. I visited with more people in more places about more things than I could begin to recall or recount. My schedule was generally conceded to have been impossible. Through it all, I saw hopes, dreams, fears, pain, pleasure, and the other million emotions that shaped Texas in this most turbulent decade.

Having just lived through this time, I decided on that sleepless night that the important story of Texas in the 1980s had to be told. This period is just too significant and historic to be put aside until a later time. In many ways, the sweeping events of the past ten years were little more than a blur of disjointed images on that seemingly endless first morning of 1990. Changes. As one who saw the ups and downs of the economy through numbers, millions of them on every nook and cranny of Texas, I knew I could offer a unique picture of what happened. But somehow I felt that a snapshot with nothing but statistics, charts, and graphs would be sterile and lifeless, not to mention boring. As one deeply involved in many of the initiatives and events that shaped the era, one who was there when the train left the station and rode the whole way, I felt my chronicle would be a credible one. As a dyed-in-the-wool Texan who lived among and talked with the people of the state on a daily basis, I knew that my story would come from the heart.

TWO

Ancient History

As I tried to put that blurred kaleidoscope of the 1980s into some sort of focus during the wee hours of the first morning of 1990, some of my thoughts inevitably drifted toward more distant times. Obviously, a new world didn't begin on January 1, 1980, any more than one began on January 1, 1990. I knew that as well as anyone. New decades bring interesting points of reference and serve as useful guideposts on an historical timeline. They also often bring us occasions to reflect on our past, present, and future; but the basic underlying structure of any economy on the first days of a new decade is rarely very different from what it was a few days before. In fact, we have to go all the way back to the early days of the exploration and settlement of this vast, untamed territory to really understand the full weight of the forces that shaped the dramatic saga of the unravelling of Texas in the 1980s.

I am not a scholar of history, and would never claim to be one. I have dabbled with the discipline off and on during my career, but never to a significant degree. In my academic writings, I have occasionally ventured a few words on the thoughts of eighteenth and nineteenth century writers and on the causes of the Great Depression. In all honesty, though, I've never had the patience to dig essential truths out of obscure and faded documents. As a part of my dissertation at Rice University, I had to take a fine-toothed comb to over twenty years worth of minutes of Federal Open Market Committee meetings. That single exercise was more than enough to convince me that history would not be my chosen profession.

Nevertheless, I do have a certain fondness for the lore of Texas in days gone by. I am also more than a little aware that a knowledge of the forces shaping the past is essential to anyone who even pretends to project the future. Forecasters who are technically competent but have no sense of the environment in which they ply their craft either find themselves with short careers or relegated to back office operations. Personally, I'd rather be out amongst the folks.

I won't try to reinvent the wheel and recount the entire story of our state in detail. There are many great writers who have chronicled the very colorful history of Texas in vivid and graphic terms. Entire books can be (and have been) written about single days. It is appropriate, however, to explore a few high points briefly from my particular vantage point as an observer of and participant in the Texas economy of the 1980s. Only by remembering and understanding some of the critical truths about our long and proud history can we hope to explore the past decade logically, or be able to look realistically toward the future of this, my native state.

The overriding lesson to be learned from our past is quite simple: Texas is not only huge physically, but is also a region that has been defined and dominated economically by its enormous natural resource endowments. Our success can be linked more to the ground than just about anything else. I used to give a speech on occasion that I called "Cattle, Cotton, and Oil," which told us a little bit about where we came from. It was a particularly relevant lesson to offer during the period immediately after the oil glut, when I was trying to convince anyone who would listen that we had to change our ways of thinking and move toward a new brand of wildcatting, one that involved mining for ideas rather than oil. My speech, laced with a healthy dose of humor, basically offered a thumbnail sketch of the three dominant industries that have taken their place of prominence in the historical development of Texas. Each had its own era of dominance, yet all remain important today. Obviously, history does not typically put a definitive period on one era and then begin a new one, be it in Rome, Greece, or Texas. Rather, epochs meld together, as did the patterns of development in the cattle, cotton, and oil industries in this rugged and bountiful land.

While cattle was clearly the first major industry in Texas, we may trace the production of cotton all the way back to the Spanish missionaries who helped settle this territory. We all know that oil spurted to prominence in the early part of this century, but let's not forget that, believe it or not, the peak in the cattle industry (in terms of number of head) came as late as 1975. Similarly, the existence of oil in Texas has been known for centuries, yet its significant influence is pretty well confined to the twentieth century. There are clearly overlaps. Nevertheless, for present purposes, it seems appropriate to consider each of these major forces in Texas as separate and distinct from one another. In that way, we can begin to see the common thread that dominated the economic history of Texas from our days as an independent republic through our heyday as the strongest state in America, and even through the eve of the turbulent 1980s. That single strand is none other than natural resources, or the economy of the ground.

Let's begin our brief economic history with cattle; after all, those enormous wild herds grazing freely through largely uncharted territory were where it all started. These beasts were the primary source of survival for settlers in a region that didn't give a lot of outward signs of future greatness. When I think of the cattle industry in Texas, I can easily conjure up many impressions that have been with me, and probably just about every other native Texan, almost since birth. I recall stories of Charles Goodnight keeping his cattle in Palo Duro Canyon, thus avoiding the need for a lengthy circle of cowhands in the days before fences. The dusty cattle trails to northern markets. TV westerns. Rustlers. Texas Rangers (including the "Lone" one), and a host of other graphic visual images. I think of barbed wire, hats, feedlots, boots with spurs, stockyards, longhorns, and the Texas-bred Santa Gertrudis. I think of the historic Y-O and King Ranches and Texas heroes of myth and legend. Just thinking about the annual September bash at the Y-O, which is still managed by direct descendents of immortal Texas Ranger Captain Charles Armand Schreiner, is enough to send chills through my spine.

The cattle industry was dominant in Texas during our period as a republic and in the early years of statehood. In fact, even prior to 1836, when we were a part of Mexico, cattle were an important aspect of Texas. Initially, the industry sprung from the fact that the animals were running wild on the vast rich grasslands of the state. It was easy enough to claim some land, round up a few head, and be in the cattle business. Later, cattle raising and transportation to northern markets became the order of the day.

By the 1850s, Texas was also emerging as a major cotton producing state. Nonetheless, the cattle industry continued to enjoy its era of dominant influence. At the close of the Civil War, the price of beef in eastern markets was three to six times as high as in Texas. We obviously figured that if our friends in other parts of the country wanted our cows that much, we'd do the neighborly thing and run 'em up there. The 1870s were a high point for the cattle drives, and Texas was generally the leading area of the country in cattle production. By the turn of the century, the number of cattle in the state stood at more than 9.4 million head. After that, increasing urbanization, new industries, and governmental policies led to a diminishing role for beef production. In fact, the total head count did not reach 10 million until the 1960s, when restrictions on cotton production brought thousands of acres of land back into use for cattle ranching.

The peak of cattle inventory in the state occurred in 1975, with well over 16 million head stomping their hooves on Texas soil. At that time, there were more cows than people. This total fell dramatically, by more than 3 million, by the latter part of the 1980s. Foreign competition, changing attitudes about beef consumption, and myriad other factors have contributed to the relative decline in our cattle industry. In some ways, cholesterol-consciousness got the best of us. But we owe cattle a lot, and we shouldn't forget it. As an industry, it was our first economic generator and remains important today. In fact, we're even learning that beef may not be so bad for us after all. As one who truly loves a good steak and once personally saw a cholesterol count of 490, I certainly hope so.

For present purposes, suffice it to say that cattle is a producing sector which originated in Texas because of our natural resource endowments. With millions of acres of unimproved land and wild herds roaming throughout the state, it was handed to us on a silver platter. Texas was not a leader in this industry to any significant degree because of our native intelligence or innate ability. Rather, it was a combination of luck, the grit of the cowboys, and, especially, the blessings of Mother Nature that spawned cattle production.

As Texas became more settled, agrarian interests turned to crops. We grew—and still grow—wheat, oats, corn, onions, sugar cane, and a variety of truck crops. We also do fairly well with strawberries, blackberries, and black-eyed peas. In the midst of all of our farming efforts, however, Cotton was King. We increased our production tenfold in the 1850s, and gradually supplanted the Old South as the dominant producer of this all-important fiber. Scarlett O'Hara was Gone With the Wind, but the Yellow Rose of Texas smelled as sweet as French perfume. Since 1880, we have been the primary producer of cotton in the United States, growing a very significant proportion (about one-third) of the total domestic output each year. It is a billion dollar industry for the state.

Our basic advantage in the early days of our cotton industry was, as with cattle, quite simple. We had enormous endowments of rich, fertile land that was newly cultivated. The rivers that traversed the territory provided the water that was needed. Unlike traditional cotton growing areas, we had not exhausted vital soil nutrients. Our yields per acre were extremely high, and we continued to make impressive gains even throughout the early part of this century. Peak levels of production occurred in 1925, when more than 18 million acres of land yielded well over 4 million bales of cotton.

The rise of new agricultural technology and efficiency has made a substantial impact on cotton production. In 1940, we picked about 2.7 million bales while farming 8.5 million acres. A quarter of a century later, we achieved slightly higher production while farming less than 4 million acres. Cotton's importance has clearly declined in recent years, reflecting greater foreign competition, preferences for other fabrics (including those horrible synthetic double-knit leisure suits that were in vogue a few years back), changing governmental policies, the continued industrialization and urbanization of the state, and the spiraling cost of agricultural production.

Nonetheless, cotton enjoyed its reign of prominence and continues to be a force in the Texas economy. Our ability to produce this valuable crop, much like our success in the cattle industry, was primarily a function of natural resource endowments. That's not to say that growing cotton is an easy job. Although machines now do most of the harvesting, a lot of folks who grew up in Texas can relate very well to picking cotton by hand. If we venture back a couple of generations, practically every citizen in the state took a turn in the fields. Despite the difficulty and genuine hard work that cotton-growing requires, our capacity to produce this important cash crop stems from fertile soil and an appropriate climate. Once again, it was the goodness of the earth that gave us our *raison d'etre.* (That's French for "reason to be." Folks tell me that you're supposed to throw one of those in every now and then when you write a book. Just be grateful that I took French at Baylor instead of Egyptian hieroglyphics.)

It may be virtually impossible to exaggerate the role cotton played in defining the Texas economy from the 1880s to about 1930. It is absolutely inconceivable that we could overstate the importance of oil during the latter stages of King Cotton's reign and most of the remainder of this century. In fact, it was the curious set of circumstances surrounding this most colorful viscous commodity that led to many of the events which characterized the turbulent 1980s. The oil economy of Texas, both directly and indirectly, became a dominant mechanism in defining a substantial part of the era of chaos that we've just survived.

Much of the attention in the past few years has clearly been directed toward banking, the thrift institutions, and real estate. When viewed in terms of dollars or any other measurable criteria, the disruptions in these sectors certainly dominate the latter portion of the past decade. They have been just about the hottest topic of discussion in the land and have grabbed the lion's share of the headlines. While some people may now be looking at the bankers and developers as the guys with the black hats, we mustn't forget that many of the seeds of their problems can be directly traced to expectations regarding future pricing and production conditions in the petroleum market. Even today, as diversification continues and other industries rise to prominence, I continue to define the alternative outlooks in our subscription forecast for Texas in terms of varying prices for this single, curious commodity. It's future and that of Texas never stray too far apart. The tensions in the Middle East that are unfolding as this book goes to press are ample evidence of that fact.

Despite its continued commanding presence these days, the petroleum industry in Texas had rather humble beginnings. No one can say with certainty when the first hints of our vast oil reserves were uncovered. The best evidence available suggests that Europeans used seepage from the soil of Texas as caulking for ships as early as 1543. It was also apparently used as a lubricant and medicinal commodity by Indians in the Nacogdoches area in the late 1700s. It was not until after the Civil War, however, that a well was actually drilled there for purposes of producing oil. (I realize that geological purists correctly maintain that oil is not "produced" except by the earth itself in an agonizingly slow process over eons, but the economist in me perpetually uses that word. If I were to name the things that distinguish economists from normal human beings, I would put our vocabulary and our Hush Puppies at the top of the list. Forgive me.) The original well, dug in the 1860s in Nacogdoches County, was followed by similar discoveries in Brown County in the late 1870s and Bexar County in the 1880s.

Back then, there was little thought that oil would become a dominant force in business activity in Texas (or anywhere else for that matter). These discoveries occurred as King Cotton was solidifying his reign. While obvious markets were developing worldwide for cotton, no one could figure out much to do with oil. From a commercial standpoint, the stuff from the Brown County field was used mostly as a lubricant and for medicinal purposes in the late 1870s. That's about the same thing the Indians were doing over in Nacogdoches almost a century earlier. Some more significant demand developed over time, as locomotives were converted from coal to oil and steamships were restructured to burn petroleum. Nonetheless, oats remained the predominant fuel for the "engines" that moved people over land. People didn't move much at all over air.

The first major field to open in Texas came about in 1894 quite by accident. While drilling a water well, some folks discovered oil in Corsicana. By 1896, this area was producing 1,450 barrels from five wells, by far the largest volume within the state. By 1900, the total had risen to more than 800,000 barrels. In the interim, the first commercially viable refinery came on line in Texas. The oil from the Corsicana field was used on streets to control dust and in the locomotives of the Houston and Texas Central Railroad Company. That early refinery produced oil for lighting and gasoline.

The strongest visual image that I have of the beginning of the oil industry in Texas is, I think, one shared by many natives. It is found in a thousand faded old photographs and dusty paintings scattered in hallways, antique stores, and albums all over the state. It is of a field near Beaumont in which an enormous gusher is spewing oil up to the sky. I'm talking, of course, about the legendary events at Spindletop, which literally erupted early in 1901. To say the least, it was a shocker. While routine drilling was interrupted to replace a bit, the roughnecks found themselves in for a lot more than they bargained for when they signed on to the crew. There was a sudden explosion of pipe, equipment, mud, rocks, and, of course, oil erupting like a volcano. Oil gushed out, as from a severed artery, for almost a week, and a bonanza of drilling activity was begun.

The detailed history of the Spindletop field has been chronicled on countless occasions, and I hesitate to repeat many of those recitations. Suffice it to say that it surpassed the Corsicana field in a few days, produced about 3.5 million barrels in 1901 and, shortly thereafter, represented one-fourth of all domestic production (about 17 million barrels) in a single year.

Four other large fields were discovered during the first decade of this century, including the legendary Humble field which produced 15 million barrels of oil in 1905. The early part of the century also saw the formation of such legendary Texas companies as Gulf, Texaco, and Humble. Along with all of the actual drilling activity, the making of the oil field equipment needed to extract this wealth of "black gold" from the ground was also emerging as a major industry in Texas. Houston was rapidly establishing itself as an oil-related manufacturing hub.

Many factors were in motion that would shape the future of the state and set the stage for the tumultuous 1980s. By that time, the old Humble Oil and Refining Company would be swallowed into giant Exxon. The 1980s would see once mighty Gulf be subjected to a famous "greenmail" raid by T. Boone Pickens before being acquired by Chevron. Texaco (the Texas Company) would transfer its headquarters to New York (that's right, New York) and, in the 1980s, fall victim to by far the biggest litigation judgment in U.S. history. Ironically, the plaintiff in this case, Pennzoil, had a name and some heritage that would suggest it should be headquartered in Pennsylvania, rather than in its impressive black edifice in downtown Houston (that's right, Houston).

None of these events were even remotely imagined, however, as the early Texas fields were coming into their own. The basic problem in the early part of the century remained the lack of demand for this gooey substance that kept surfacing in such abundance. We kept finding the stuff almost in spite of ourselves, but nobody could quite figure out what to do with it. In fact, while Spindletop was spewing millions of barrels into the market, the price fell to only 3¢ per barrel.

Signs of change in this situation were, however, already beginning to surface in Detroit, Kitty Hawk, and other places of historical note. As automobiles and airplanes began to roll onto and above the landscape, the demand for oil and, indeed, the entire character of the petroleum sector changed dramatically. By 1915, it was apparent that substantial markets for petroleum products were indeed being established. Oats and buggy whips were giving way to the amazing black liquid oozing from pools far below the surface of Texas.

The oil industry in Texas experienced another dramatic turn of events in October of 1930. The Depression was gripping the farmers of East Texas, not to mention the dust bowl disaster. The lack of available credit was severely threatening their very existence.

Most of these folks knew very little about Wall Street, but they knew their own reality. About the only way to get a bank to part with any money in those days was to encourage the withdrawal with a gun, a feat which an infamous Texas couple named Bonnie Parker and Clyde Barrow turned into an almost noble science. A significant group of diligent tillers of the East Texas soil, though, were saved in more legal and completely natural ways. Kilgore was the site of what was, at the time, far and away the largest pool of oil discovered in the entire history of the petroleum industry. As one who grew up a generation or so later only a few miles away, the stories of that time and place are second nature to me. For those of you not so fortunate, a visit to the East Texas Oil Museum in Kilgore is well worth the trip, particularly if you fortify yourself while you're there with some ribs at the Country Tavern. Before my cholesterol level approached the land speed record, I tasted ribs all over the country, and, indeed, the world; there are none finer.

When it comes to this historic field, the numbers are truly startling. By July of 1931, more than 3,000 wells had been drilled. Peak production in 1933 was more than 200 million barrels, an amount which exceeded that of the rest of the state combined. In October of 1931, there was one week in which an average of more than one well per hour came into existence. Thousands of people poured into Kilgore and brought with them the new economy of East Texas.

The story of the Kilgore field is the stuff of good novels. The price of domestic crude oil fell from about a dollar a barrel to about a dime in the course of only a few months. At one point, it is said that the price of a bucket of water in Kilgore exceeded that of a bucket of oil. Given the heat and humidity of summers in East Texas, that piece of lore is certainly within the bounds of reason. A classic struggle between the major producers and small independents ensued. Marshall law ruled the day, production quotas were imposed, and all of the other trappings of a great economic and political human drama unfolded. The fact that the governor of the state at the time was one of the founders of Humble certainly didn't detract from the excitement in any way. You've probably already figured out which side he was on.

The 1940s, '50s, and '60s brought steady increases in crude production within the state. During much of this period, an average of 3,000 new wells were brought in annually. Needless to say, the economy became heavily dependent on oil in every way. As the 1970s ran their course, production patterns began to gradually, at times almost imperceptibly, decline. The proven reserves had not even begun to be exhausted, but much of the "easy" oil had been retrieved.

There were dramatic events to occur in this decade, however, that would make the modest drop in production pale into almost total insignificance. Major international forces were rapidly leading to a situation which would produce one of the greatest economic windfalls Texas or any other state had ever experienced. Whether you call it the "energy crisis" or the "oil boom" is nothing more than a reflection of where you live. The incredible twists and turns in the oil market of the 1970s are inextricably linked with the business situation in Texas in the 1980s. Manufacturing, banking, and just about everything else in the state would hitch its horse to the rising star that was petroleum.

Cattle, cotton, and oil. I used that phrase countless times in my speeches around the state. As I sought to describe the old Texas economy and the emerging new Texas economy, that combination held the key to the past. If you say "cattle, cotton, and oil" rapidly enough, you discover that it becomes very difficult. More than once my tongue was tied on the phrase. Regardless of how hard it was to say, the one thing I never lost sight of was what it meant for our economy.

When cattle was dominant, we had enormous advantages in that industry which were tied to our natural resource base. When cotton was dominant, the same phenomenon surfaced. Obviously, the enormous petroleum reserves found under the vast agricultural lands of Texas were also a product of natural endowments.

In short, the original engines that drove the Texas economy of the past were deeply rooted in our accidental good fortune. We plucked our prosperity from the plums of nature. People worked hard, people were innovative, and some, although certainly not everyone, got very, very rich. Yet we can never forget that much of the economic success of Texas was tied to its location, climate, soil, and minerals.

There is certainly nothing wrong with this pattern in our economic history. In fact, the simple principle of comparative advantage plays a role in many aspects of economic activity, as well it should. The lesson to be learned from this panorama lies in the fact that industralization and technological progress have now reached a point at which we can no longer rely exclusively, or even primarily, on the bounty of the earth. The emphasis must shift to the far more fruitful and infinite bounty of the mind. Simply stated, the new growth industries of the future are not likely to be linked to the ground. Obviously, we can create comparative advantages for ourselves in the modern technological economy. In fact, as I will comment upon later, our success in this regard to date has been notable. The critical difference is that we must now proactively and aggressively work to create many of our advantages. We can't simply sit back and wait for Mother Nature to bring them to us.

While cattle, cotton, and oil will continue to be a part of our economy for the foreseeable future, we can no longer rely on them as our fundamental propelling forces. Our natural resource endowments will always be an important source of economic advantage to us, but they must now be complemented to a much more significant degree by creative human endeavors. It is in this context that we can view the triumphant peaks of the 1970s and the devastating valleys of the 1980s as transitional forces for shaping the "conquering" economy of the 1990s and beyond.

THREE

The Oil Boom

No one can understand the 1980s in Texas without first getting a sense of what happened in the 1970s. Many events from the distant and near past combine to shape any situation. The forces of nature that brought Texas through its formative years are linked to the 1980s and the period beyond. It is the immediate past, however, that often gives us our best clues to a dramatic turn of events. Viewed in this manner, much of the real story of the 1980s in Texas can begin appropriately in about 1973. Other strains and subplots can be traced all the way back into the reaches of time, but the dynamics that led up to the turbulent swings of the 1980s clearly have their genesis in the great Texas "oil boom."

As 1973 began, many events were making headlines; events which would later shape the destiny of the state in ways that we couldn't begin to perceive at the time. There were rumblings about potential gas shortages and an energy crisis before the year began, but little was made of them. Prices were restrained by the wage and price controls that had been imposed by President Nixon in 1971. Several centuries of attempts at such artificial constraints suggest that the concept doesn't work for very long, but each generation seems determined to give it one more try.

As a result, America continued to run on cheap energy. We were well past the point that Texas could supply the needs of the nation. We obtained quite a bit of it from faraway lands, with political and economic interests that rarely coincided with our own. It doesn't take a degree in rocket science to figure out that if you keep the domestic price of petroleum below the levels dictated by the world market, we'll use too much of it. When that happens, we give the countries that supply us with oil enormous control over our daily lives.

Ironically, the actual production of Texas oil peaked in 1972, which was a year before the great bonanza began. This fact merely shows that the number of barrels brought to the market is determined much more by geology than economics. If we could have coaxed more oil out of the ground and into the gas pumps during the rest of the 1970s, you better believe that we would have. At one point before all was said and done, we had more than 1,400 drilling rigs poking holes in Texas ground at the same time. They were all trying to seize the moment and force more of that lucrative black stuff to the surface.

Over the next eight years, there were dramatic increases in prices, approaching $40 per barrel at the peak. Despite this more than tenfold rise in prices, the number of barrels produced and delivered to the market from the Lone Star State remarkably never regained the 1972 level.

One interesting point is worth noting here. At the end of 1972, the rotary rig count in the state, the weekly barometer of drilling activity to which Texas-watchers are slavishly addicted, reached 372. This marked the highest level in three years, yet that same number of operating rigs would be regarded as indicative of a massive slump only a few short years later. There were signs of an imminent surge in the industry. As 1973 began, Lone Star Gas announced grandiose plans to spend $95 million on construction and $340 million on oil exploration over the course of the year. At about the same time, Exxon announced record fourth quarter earnings of almost $500 million.

I must confess that my own activities at the eve of the "oil boom" were not focused very intently on the Texas economy. I was far more concerned with my own economy. I was an undergraduate mathematics student at Baylor University recovering from an automobile accident that I had suffered in December of 1972. I had fallen victim to one of those erratic and unpredictable Texas ice storms. As 1973 began, I was much more enamored with my new yellow Mustang than I was with any of the major events shaping future business conditions. That car stayed with me pretty much throughout the entire oil boom, and I must confess that my driving habits with that big V-8 engine didn't do much to encourage fuel economy. When it came time to take my picture for the jacket of this book, I insisted that it be with another kind of Mustang—one of those impressive beasts occupying center stage at Las Colinas. I greatly admire both the artistry of the sculptor and the elegant grace and enormous strength of the animal. To me, those magnificent wild horses are simultaneously an embodiment of the glory of Texas past, the excesses underlying our recent difficulties, and the hope and power of our future. If I were totally honest about it, however, I would probably have to admit that at least part of my motivation was a subtle and subconscious tribute to that old, endearing vehicle from my past.

If I was focused on anything in 1973 that extended beyond my own little universe, it was on the unfolding Watergate scandal. I kept pretty close tabs on President Nixon's Waterloo in Washington. I was also watching the winding down of the conflict in Vietnam, grateful that my number had not come up but well aware of my friends who had responded to the call.

I had no way of knowing that forces were surfacing in Texas that would generate events that I would be pulled into in significant ways a decade or so later. It also never occurred to me that I was watching the beginnings of one of the most explosive economic periods that my native state would ever experience. My biggest problems were confined to the textbook and the pocket book.

On January 1, 1973, First National Bank of Dallas announced the formation of First International Bancshares. This multi-bank holding company would join several others in the state in an aggressive era of acquisitions and growth. No one could have dreamed then, even in his worst nightmare, that First International would (1) later adopt the name InterFirst, (2) merge with its arch rival, Republic, into an entity known as First RepublicBank, and (3) take on yet another identity, that of NCNB Texas, as the hard times took their toll in the late 1980s. The very thought of a bank from North Carolina owning the largest financial organization within the state was beyond the realm of even remote possibility in 1973. A whole series of laws steeped in the Populist heritage of Texas would have to be scrapped. Two distinct corporate cultures, the aggressive tradition of First National and the staid, traditional Dallas properness of Republic, would have to be forged into an alliance. A short while later, a huge infusion of federal funds would have to be brought to the table. But all of that would happen, in a very different Texas at a very different time than on the initial day of 1973.

Back then, the bank holding companies of Texas were considerably restricted in their capacity to expand. Every acquisition was subjected to rigid scrutiny to determine its competitive effects—not just on the affected local area, but on the whole state! Interstate ownership and branching were strictly prohibited. Even Automated Teller Machines (ATMs) were considered branches and, thus, not permitted. Attitudes (and regulations) regarding the size of holding companies, branch banking, and interstate banking would have to undergo radical changes before any of the major steps on the road to NCNB Texas could be taken. In the course of the next decade and a half, they would. In spades. Necessity can be the mother not only of invention, but also legislation, regulation, and an occasional attitude adjustment.

Even though I was just an undergraduate student at the time, I did have one firsthand opportunity to observe the nature of Texas bank holding companies at this critical juncture. I must say, though, that I certainly had no idea I would ultimately become involved in task forces, litigation, bankruptcies, real estate evaluation, and other serious matters related to these institutions. My brush with the future of Texas banking came in the fall semester of 1973. As part of a research class, I visited First National Bank of Dallas, the "flagship" bank of the newly-minted First International Bancshares. (Flagships are what they were called back in those days. The shipwrecks would come later.)

I was about to embark on a project to determine what type of loan participations might be possible if they were to purchase a bank in the Waco area. It ended up as primarily a theoretical exercise; this particular acquisition was ultimately thwarted in the wild and wooly world of Texas politics. Nonetheless, this class assignment gave me a good initial glimpse of the aggressive operating nature that prevailed in Texas banking at the time, although certainly not a large enough one to allow me to foresee the dramatic events that were to unfold over the next few years. It was also my first occasion to meet Jim Byrd, the legendary economic guru of First National. He was courteous, friendly, and made quite an impression on a kid who was beginning to ponder the possibility of going to graduate school in economics.

As I said earlier, the dominant thoughts in my life in 1973 had little to do with the economy. I was a young mathematics major and realized that I had a certain affinity for the intricate puzzles of economics. In many ways, however, my interests and skills had not yet left the pages of the textbooks. My energies, in addition to studying, were trained on trying to earn enough money to keep my head above water, while planning to marry a young lady from Magnolia, Texas by the name of Nancy Satterwhite. We both had several years of school ahead of us and had little clue of what was in store as we tried to earn our keep and pursue our education. We tied the knot on a hot day in July; then we worried about how to go about eating.

Although I was never very good at such things (I'm still not), Nancy and I made valiant attempts to construct a budget that would somehow stretch my income from a scholarship and a couple of part-time jobs into our own brand of survival. We tried to estimate all of our costs in a very dutiful manner, discussed how romantic it would be to starve together, and went along in the vague hope that the wage and price controls would somehow insulate us from too many unexpected variations in our budget. Little did we know that shortly after we were married, all sorts of crazy things would happen to prices in the economy. By then, we were into the various phases of the decontrol of wages and prices, and the folks who sold stuff just couldn't wait to mark up the stickers. Beef and chicken prices would rise, but we already figured that we couldn't afford to eat much anyway. However, living in Waco at the time, we did plan to do a lot of driving.

If Waco was recognized for anything in the early 1970s, it was renowned for its ferocious gas wars. (We were also known for a particularly bad football team at Baylor, but Coach Grant Teaff came along and changed all of that!) Prices below 20¢ per gallon at the pump were quite common. I have often said that the price in Waco at that time barely covered the federal and state excise taxes. Basically, the stations gave the gasoline away in the hopes that you would buy a soft drink, a bag of peanuts, or something else so that they could make a little money. (Sometimes, this approach worked pretty well: there are more than a few Texans who wouldn't think of drinking a soda water without first dumping a bag of peanuts in it.)

That picture changed abruptly before 1973 ended. An oil embargo and related production cuts would put upward pressure on gasoline prices and severely restrict availability. Even though Texas was still producing waterfalls of the stuff, scarcities abounded. By this point in history, our market power was overshadowed by the sheiks in the Middle East. On a personal note, Nancy and I would find ourselves unable to buy the one commodity we thought we could afford as a poor young couple living in Waco. Much to our shock and dismay, we couldn't afford to drive or eat. Hence, my first brush with what most of the nation calls the energy crisis was not at all pleasant. I had the unfortunate circumstance, like so many others, to be a consumer rather than a producer of oil. That fact served to complicate my life considerably at the time. Little did I realize what a blessing those gas lines and spiraling prices around the country were to good ol' Texas. I also didn't see the utter simplicity of defining the "haves" and the "have nots" of the economic universe.

There were other major events unfolding that would shape the future of Texas as 1973 began. On the first day of the new year, that great old Texas company by the name of Humble Oil and Refining became Exxon USA, swallowed in a corporate gulp. Ironically, shortly after that, an old man by the name of Curt Hammell died. He was the last of that special group of roughnecks who brought in the Spindletop gusher (or, at least, got out of the way while it exploded) in 1901. As Mr. Hammell died at the age of 100, history managed to link the origination of one spurt in oil activity to the onset of another.

Among the other events of 1973 that would affect the future of our state in many ways were (1) a new announcement regarding superconductivity from the Tennessee Valley Authority, (2) Southwest Airlines' decision to fly from Dallas Love Field, (3) the inauguration of the Dallas/Fort Worth (DFW) International Airport, and (4) initial signs that a giant real estate development known as Las Colinas would be created from scratch out of the vast vacant space near the new airport. The Mustangs of Las Colinas were not yet a reality, but my little yellow one was purring along fine. There was also discussion of a possible nuclear power plant in North Texas, to be known as Comanche Peak.

Of far more immediate significance were the troubling developments in the Middle East. That one really got everyone's attention—especially in Texas. The news was full of rumblings regarding oil shortages. Congress even held hearings on the topic as early as April and May. Posted oil prices remained around $3 per barrel for most of the year, but spot market activity zoomed upwards, indicating that much higher petroleum costs were on the horizon. Holiday shortages of fuel became a source of concern over Memorial Day weekend. Indeed, people were beginning to notice.

Texas was certainly not immune to these shortages. At one point early in the year, Dallas was a dog's hair away from running out of fuel. The University of Texas at Austin was forced to close many classroom buildings for lack of heating fuel. By late spring, FINA could not operate its stations on Sundays. In May, San Antonio had to adopt drastic conservation measures, including curtailment of lights in offices and on the streets. The city was down to only a 10-day supply of energy. And in June, Governor Dolph Briscoe even reduced the lighting on state highways. Then there was the nationally mandated 55 mile-per-hour speed limit and those aggravating lines at gas stations. I'm sure anybody old enough to drive back then has some sort of war story about the situation. All of this hoopla was taking place in a state where driving 100 miles or more for a steak dinner was considered an inalienable right. It also wasn't supposed to take much more than an hour to get there.

The situation was complicated even further by enormous political tensions in the Middle East. Things reached a critical point in early October of 1973, with the outbreak of the Yom Kippur War. This event led the Organization of Arab Petroleum Exporting Countries (OAPEC) to seek a substantial embargo on oil to countries identified as "hostile" to Arab interests. Because of long-standing U.S. support for Israel, we made the bad list. In mid-October, the embargo began. It included outright cancellation of shipments to selected countries (including the United States) and cuts in production across the board. Posted prices rose from $3 a barrel to more than $5 a barrel almost instantaneously.

The embargo only lasted for about five months, and was officially ended in mid-March of the following year. As far as embargoes go, it will probably not receive very high marks from history. Transshipment (passing the stuff through another country) and a dozen other techniques to get around the problem pervaded the entire period, and petroleum produced in the Arab world continued steadily to make its way to the United States. There were significant increases in oil prices, and considerable world attention was focused on the embargo itself. In reality, however, these rises were a result of the production cuts rather than the poorly executed and unenforceable embargo on particular nations. In essence, the exporting nations of the world were capitalizing on the same economic principles that had driven the actions of the Texas Railroad Commission four decades earlier. By controlling a significant portion of the known world supply of oil, as the Railroad Commission had at one point in Texas, these countries evolved a capacity to heavily influence price in a manner that could yield them a substantial amount of money (at least for a while).

As time progressed, the market made rational responses to higher oil prices. Markets have a habit of doing that. New exploration brought in new discoveries, fuel substitution and alternate energy sources became more plausible, consumers began conserving energy, and new equipment was designed to be more fuel efficient. Even the automobile, the one arena where all of America traditionally agreed with Texas that bigger was better, became a lot smaller. Gas-hogging V-8 engines became almost like dinosaurs. As a result, the power base of the Arab countries and, in fact, the whole of the larger and more widely known Organization of Petroleum Exporting Countries (OPEC), was mightily diluted. Such is the way of cartels that cannot control all aspects of supply and must function within a market environment. In the early 1970s, however, OPEC had its day, and the power to leverage the world with oil prices was clearly present.

The embargo (or, more properly, the production cuts) had tremendous impacts, both real and symbolic. By the end of 1973, the United States would find itself in the midst of its longest and most serious recession in several decades. It would not end until 1975. Significant impacts were also experienced in Western Europe, the Pacific Rim, and other places around the globe that were net importers of petroleum. It was definitely not a good time to be buying oil.

With prices soaring, it is not surprising that virtually any place that was a net exporter or seller of oil would benefit enormously. Texas, of course, was one of those places. Despite high interest rates, high inflation, and other factors which universally rose their ugly heads from the combined mess of a national recession and the gradual removal of wage and price guidelines, Texas managed largely to avert the recession. The prosperity of the oil industry was sufficient to overcome the other difficulties which inevitably accompany a national recession. Simply stated, Texas is a huge seller of petroleum. *Ipso facto,* when the price goes up, the state is a net winner.

The numbers tell a compelling story of the economic explosion that occurred in Texas from 1973 through 1981. I don't want to go into a lot of detail, but you have to look at a few of the basic facts to really appreciate just how unprecedented this spree of expansion really was. As the U.S. entered its severe contraction, Texas found itself faced with unparalleled growth opportunities. The price of oil would double again and again over the next eight years. The price of a barrel of West Texas Intermediate crude would approach $40 at times before the "oil boom" ran its course. The national economy, on the other hand, would experience substantial difficulties for much the same reason. The recession of 1973-1975 was followed by a mild downturn in 1979, which again can be traced largely to oil market factors. As the 1980s began, the country slid into a recession that was actually worse than that experienced in the mid-1970s. Once again, petroleum prices were the primary culprit.

The status of the economy was clearly the number one concern in the minds of all Americans by the beginning of the 1980s. It ranked at the top of every opinion poll. Presidential candidate Ronald Reagan was able to win a landslide victory over incumbent President Jimmy Carter, in large measure because of economic conditions. Reagan, in one of the early slick public relations coups of the type that would characterize his entire administration, successfully combined the national unemployment rate and the inflation rate to create a much-publicized measure called the "Misery Index," a label which captured the very essence of national attitudes at the time.

In Texas, though, the Index could be measured more in terms of merriment than misery. Throughout this period, Texas was growing, counter to the rest of the country, in an altogether dramatic fashion. Here are the numbers. From 1973 through 1981, personal income virtually tripled. Retail sales gains were almost equally impressive. The state gained more than 2.2 million jobs, a 40% increase. In 1973, the population of Texas stood at 12 million people, a figure that it had taken the state its entire history to achieve. By the time the oil boom ran its course, our population exceeded 15 million folks. The real gross state product of Texas advanced 40% in just the six years between 1975 and 1981. Real output rose by 9.4% in 1981 alone. And remember, all of this was happening during an era in which the national economy was experiencing parts of three recessions and was limping along at a very sluggish pace. Misery may love company, but Texas wasn't making any plans to join that crowd.

The real telling numbers came between 1979 and 1982. Those years exemplified the difference between us and the rest of the country at that point in history; it was the height of national economic difficulties on the one hand, and the height of prosperity for Texas on the other. In fact, there were even some recessionary forces beginning for us in 1982, as I've described briefly, brought on mostly by an oil glut. Despite this fact, however, the overall numbers for this four-year period are little short of unbelievable.

From 1979 to 1982, the gross national product of the United States was virtually unchanged. In fact, it actually declined by $26 billion. I know that seems like a lot to folks like us, but it's only a fraction of a percent of our multi-trillion dollar national output. I have often referred to that period as "the great national roller coaster ride." The U.S. economy went up, down, all around, sideways, and took some strange curves. Gross national product plunged by more than 9% on an annualized basis in a single quarter. It also rose by a comparable amount in another quarter. The prime interest rate also jumped around in an incredible fashion, and inflation and unemployment ran rampant. Despite all these twists and turns, the nation ended up, like a roller coaster, at the same place where it began. While the country rode this roller coaster, Texas boarded a fast train. During those four crazy years, the U.S. as a whole experienced that net loss of $26 billion in gross national product, or output, and 200,000 jobs, while our state alone had a net gain of $43 billion in output and 800,000 new jobs. Just think what the country's numbers would have been like if Texas hadn't been around.

Needless to say, the world began to sit up and take notice of Texas. Our economic prosperity, achieved in the midst of almost global business chaos, made us the living, breathing symbol of prosperity to the entire Free World. Texas managed to capture the imagination of just about everyone. Around the globe, fashion turned to boots, cowboy hats, and jeans, preferably made in Texas. Country and Western music, most notably the Austin sound, swept the planet as well. Willie Nelson and Waylon Jennings had everybody talking about moving to Luckenbach. The Dallas Cowboys were, believe it or not, "America's team." These gridiron namesakes of another era in Texas couldn't lose (except maybe when the Pittsburgh Steelers showed up; even then, the people loved them). Their stoical coach, Tom Landry, was a national icon. Even the Cowboy cheerleaders were international celebrities. The other Texas entry in the National Football League was the gridiron namesake of the dominant industry of the day, the Houston Oilers. The Oilers also had their day in the sunshine, as running back Earl Campbell (who was named for and delivered by the same physician who had assisted at the birth of a future short economist a few years earlier) became the literal embodiment of athletic strength and prowess.

Southwestern art and artifacts enjoyed an incredible revival. Movies like "Urban Cowboy" were box office smashes. There was also a cult hit named "The Texas Chainsaw Massacre," but maybe that's another story! The biggest thing on television was the quintessential evening soap, "Dallas." As the show's Neilsen ratings soared, we all waited anxiously throughout a blistering summer to learn "Who shot J.R.?"

This euphoria over Texas had profound implications. It brought into play a basic notion that has come to be known as Ray's Law of Economics: The Most Important Thing is What People Think. There is little doubt that the "oil boom" affected what people thought about the Lone Star State. The world decided that we were wonderful, if maybe a little arrogant. Those of us in Texas, for the most part, thought we were invincible and we acted that way. Our air of perpetual superiority was fueled (pardon the pun, please!) by the anticipation of a never ending upward spiral in the price of our precious and vital commodity. Belief can indeed be a powerful narcotic. The unyielding convictions regarding invulnerability, brought on by a long and uninterrupted "boom" in the face of global chaos, set the stage for much of what happened in the 1980s.

Beyond oil and its attendant explosion, there were many other things happening in Texas during the magnificent growth spree of the 1970s. Some of them were key to the overall saga, while others were merely interesting and at times highly publicized sidelights. For example, it became apparent shortly before the oil embargo ended that certain members of the flamboyant and fabulously wealthy Hunt family were trying to corner the world silver market. This tale of high-stakes market manipulation and its attendant court battles would be played out for years to come. By the time it ended in the late 1980s, the Hunt brothers involved wouldn't be quite as poor as church mice, but they sure would end up sitting on a precarious bench of seriously shrunken assets.

It was during 1974 that First National Bank of Dallas openly intensified its long-standing rivalry with Republic Bank of Dallas, and temporarily passed Republic in asset size. By 1975, the operating rig count within the state rested at an eleven-year high of 630, but the best was yet to come. In the mid-'70s, Dallas became the first digitally-switched city in Southwestern Bell's telephone network. By the end of the 1980s, I would be intensely absorbed in a concerted effort to extend this technology to even the most rural segments of the Bell System. In so doing, I would be made to realize just how cumbersome the regulatory process has become.

In 1975, a major study rated Houston, Dallas, and Fort Worth as the top three cities in the country in terms of future job prospects. The latter half of the decade was replete with announcements of remarkable growth in the performance of the state's banks and savings and loan associations (S&Ls). Texas financial institutions were frequently ranked among the top performers in the nation, with rates of return that far exceeded industry norms. Banks were aggressively hiring young business school graduates, and unrestrained energy lending was propping up balance sheets and income statements in remarkable ways. Loans to less developed countries (LDCs) in Latin America were also becoming quite popular. After all, some of these places also had substantial oil reserves, and oil would take care of everything.

Although the explosive building boom that would bring Texas almost to its knees in the near future had not yet begun, there were already numerous reports of our healthy real estate markets. Dallas and Houston were commonly listed among the leaders in the nation. It was, of course, the banks and S&Ls, aided by a healthy dose of new tax and financial legislation, that fueled the real estate frenzy that, along with sluggish demand, led to the real estate bust that led, with the help of a few other things, to the bank bust . . . but more on that later.

By this point, near the end of the blissful 1970s, I was a young economist just getting started on my career and writing a lot of highly technical critiques of U.S. monetary policy from the vantage of my academic ivory tower. (Actually it was a concrete basement, but everybody has to start somewhere.) Little did I know that, a decade later, much of my time would be devoted to working on the cleanup of banking and real estate matters in Texas (and most other parts of the nation). The events that were about to occur (and my role in them) would lead me to spend a lot of time in task force meetings, legislative hearings, and all types of legal proceedings. There were instances in which I was moving back and forth between the ivory tower and the asphalt jungle so quickly that it is at least a minor miracle that I didn't bump my head.

As the decade drew to a close, it was anticipated that two major nuclear plants, the Comanche Peak Plant in Glen Rose and the South Texas Project in Bay City, would open in the early 1980s. These impressive and thoroughly modern facilities were supposed to help provide the juice to satiate the ravenous appetites of burgeoning industrial development in the Dallas-Fort Worth Metroplex and along the oil dependent Texas Gulf Coast. In the aftermath of the near-catastrophe at Three Mile Island, and a rapidly evolving and complex regulatory process, I would find myself working on information regarding the initial commercial use of these plants even into the 1990s. Both facilities became mired in complexities that repeatedly delayed their implementation. In the meantime, some of the growth expectations that were their genesis failed to materialize.

There were more things happening in the latter part of the 1970s. In 1978, Texas elected its first Republican governor since Reconstruction, Bill Clements, who would also be a major force in Texas in the 1980s. That same year, LTV, a giant Texas company that began in a garage in Dallas, was involved in activities with its steel subsidiaries that would lead to my first major experience in the litigation system a few years later. At various times during the saga of this massive conglomerate, it would own Braniff, Wilson Sporting Goods, Wilson Meats, steel companies, aerospace operations, and electronics subsidiaries, to name but a few. Texas Instruments announced the remarkable 64K memory microchip, which, with its even more powerful successors, would revolutionize the way our world functions. American Airlines announced that it was moving its headquarters to Dallas from New York. The year 1978 also saw the Shah make his exit from Iran, leaving this already volatile country in complete chaos. It was the end of both a powerful dynasty and a way of life for U.S. diplomacy in the Middle East. In Bonham, Texas, a small company that makes gas pumps added a digit to their price screens to reflect the imminent arrival of gasoline marked at over a dollar per gallon.

As the decade ended, Texas was indeed riding high. One newspaper article regarding the Dallas/Fort Worth area described the local economic outlook as "cloudless." John Connally was announcing with great fanfare that he was a candidate for president. Forecasts were calling for higher and higher oil prices, with the phrase "$85 in '85" being frequently trumpeted. The notion of oil selling for $85 per barrel by 1985 seemed a little optimistic, but by no means farfetched. Many of the major oil companies had projections for prices in the $70+ per barrel range at the time. Even if you took a pessimistic look at the situation, such as through the eyes of a "conservative" banker or a budget-conscious legislator, you would probably come up with something along the lines of $60. No one was even thinking that the dream of "$85 in '85" would become the harsh reality of "$10 in '86." Many cities in Texas and elsewhere adopted "odd/even" gasoline purchasing programs, limits on the number of gallons purchased, and other remedies for inadequate supplies. Although the nation was suffering a very sluggish downturn, Texas was experiencing an economic surge of monumental proportions.

Perhaps more important than what was actually happening were the expectations about what would happen. As I said earlier, the prevailing attitude of the time was strong and simple. Prospects were boundless, growth would continue, and "recession proof" was a phrase often applied to Texas. Economies are driven by what people think—nothing more, nothing less. The environment was ripe for something to happen. What people thought was about to be at serious odds with the emerging storm of international tensions, governmental policies, and private sector excesses.

As a minor appendage to this whole set of activity, there was a young, fairly short economist in Waco who had begun building an econometric model of the state of Texas. You guessed it—me. I began the process in late 1978 or early 1979. (There was no particular reason to memorialize the date at the time.) Believe me, we started with very meager resources. There was no staff, except for a few student volunteers, my wife (in an uncompensated capacity), and a very adept student assistant by the name of Leigh Humphrey (now Martinez), who has been my business partner ever since. Material was begged and borrowed from a variety of places, computer facilities were inadequate, library resources were limited, and there was no budget. I almost had to chuck the whole project because of the strains it was putting on my personal financial resources. What was happening in Texas seemed to hold my interest a whole lot more than "Fed watching." Later, of course, my experience in the realm of monetary policy and institutions would serve me well as federal banking and thrift regulators began to take more than a passing interest in Texas. It seems that everything I've done in my entire life came together in a remarkable way to keep me in the middle of everything. I can't begin to tell you how grateful I am for the opportunity.

I definitely had ambitions, and, like everything else I've ever jumped into, I poured myself intensely into the effort. I'll be the first to admit, however, that I had no idea where I was heading with my model. In fact, at that point, it was generally pretty easy to forecast the economy of Texas. In essence, you just projected a big growth rate and hoped you weren't too low. However, by the time I finally finished the initial phase of the model and released my first forecast a few years later, I would be projecting an altogether different scenario. What I saw—and predicted publicly—was a downturn, not just in oil and gas extraction, but in manufacturing as well. It was an insight that practically put my Texas citizenship in jeopardy.

The primary focus of this story is clearly on the 1980s. In order to have an understanding of the major events within the '80s, however, it was imperative that we talk about at least the high points of the 1970s. It was the "oil boom" that led to some of the turbulence of the 1980s. Although not clearly foreseen at the time, many of the forces that would shape the 1980s were already in place (or at least getting there).

As we've just talked about, the economic landscape of Texas was indeed rich and fertile. Our prospects seemed excellent and, from the perspective of virtually every observer, there was little, if any, downside on the horizon. My own perspective at the time was overwhelmingly technical. I was still in the trenches building an econometric model. I didn't have the staff of outstanding professionals that surround me today. I had not yet released a forecast or begun my all-important effort of being "out and about" to investigate major economic patterns and events from the inside. I was preoccupied by computer programs, and my visions were of simulation algorithms, autoregressive disturbances, multicollinearity, simultaneous equation estimators, varying parameters, dynamic systems theory, and conditions for stability in non-linear stochastic processes. (Sounds fascinating, huh?)

Believe it or not, those things really are important to what I do, and I've written more than a few obtuse academic articles and books about them. (My collected academic papers now number twenty-or-so volumes, each about three inches thick.) The reams of computer output and strings of mathematical formulas pale in comparison, however, to the knowledge one gains as a keen observer and active participant in the process. That's not to say that millions of numbers and equations that come within my purview each day are not vitally important. Indeed, they are essential. I wouldn't have the structural basis or analytical foundations for what I do without them. Nevertheless, the "rubber meets the road" on the track where the race is run. I must confess, though, that these "real world" issues were far from my mind as I laboriously pieced together the first version of the intricate mathematical puzzle that became my Texas model. Needless to say, for me and for Texas, the 1980s were going to let loose a whole bagful of surprises.

FOUR

The '80s in a Nutshell

Texas has just lived through the most tumultuous decade since the Great Depression, if not, in some fundamental ways, of our entire history. The 1980s were almost beyond belief. A confluence of forces lined up to create a seemingly endless stream of complete economic chaos. We can tell the story in terms of virtually any numbers that we choose, although in reality it is much more a story of people and events than numbers.

Fortunes were lost. Texas legends toppled. Financial institutions were brought to their knees. Real estate deals collapsed in droves. Businesses went belly up. Job losses were at times measured in the hundreds of thousands. Some giant corporations went bankrupt or were swallowed up in mega-mergers. I am going to spend much of the rest of this treatise going through the 1980s in detail. Before doing that, however, I decided I should give you a quick synopsis. Otherwise, we might all lose perspective.

When oil prices collapsed in the mid-1980s, more than 200,000 people lost their jobs in Houston alone. That's like putting the entire workforce of Alaska out of a job at once. Our friendly neighbor to the far north may be bigger than Texas geographically, but we've gained and lost a lot more workers than they've ever had many times over the past decade. (Sometimes the "Texas brag" comes out in the strangest ways and places.) These were not just any jobs, either. A good portion of the unemployed came from high-paying occupations in the oil patch; others were skilled manufacturing workers, the backbone of our key export sectors. The massive layoffs and plant closures were followed by a slowdown in service sector businesses. If you're out of work, you don't need your clothes cleaned quite so often, and you certainly don't dine as much in fancy restaurants. Toward the end of the period, bankers, construction workers, and real estate brokers took their turns in the proverbial bread lines as well.

People walked away from mortgages, packing their possessions and moving out of modest first homes and celestial mansions alike in the middle of the night. In many cases, those who turned in the keys, or even stayed around to sell their homes for a loss, were abandoning the only real asset that they had. The equity of a lifetime vanished in a moment, as the American Dream suddenly became the Texas Nightmare. Other people were hanging on by their fingernails, many of which had only a short while ago been freshly manicured on a weekly basis.

Texans, who had come through the previous decade unscathed and justifiably proud, weren't at all prepared for the free fall that our economy took in the 1980s. People from small towns and big cities, finding their security stripped away from them, simply couldn't fathom the enormous game in which they found themselves as pawns. As they faced the loss of gainful employment, self esteem, and assets, their thoughts turned to immediate matters. There was neither the time nor the inclination to ponder the vast forces beyond their own limited world view that were ulitmately responsible for their pain and suffering. Basically, they just wanted to eat.

The story of what happened, and why, has been called complex and almost incomprehensible by many; in reality, it is very straightforward and understandable. It involves nothing more than my basic Law of Economics. This single, concise rule is unequivocal. What people think drives all economic behavior! When expectations and reality coincide, everything works fine. When they don't, things can get real messed up. In that context, Texas in the '80s is a story that is simple to tell, but by no means easy. As I stared again and again at the numbers that defined the 1980s, I was fully aware that they represented not just figures on a page but living, breathing people. Day after day I saw brutal statistics that told of lost money, lost jobs, and lost opportunities. As I traveled tens of thousands of miles and talked to tens of thousands of people each month, I met many of the actual individuals who were reflected in the seemingly endless shower of negative numbers.

As I went out to help communities with economic development initiatives, I could sense a mood of quiet desperation and utter confusion about what was happening to them. At times, it seemed as if all I could do was offer a little hope about the future. I'm sure it was at one of those moments that the diversification of the state's economic base and the creation of new employment opportunities became an absolute obsession with me. I wanted to take an aggressive and proactive role in improving these disturbing numbers that I had to look at, analyze, and, yes, even shake hands with every day.

In a nutshell, here's what happended. We roared into the '80s on the crest of the great oil boom, and the momentum of that juggernaut kept going as the "boom" became a bust. By 1982, the oil glut had begun. The banks that had prospered mightily from energy lending found themselves in trouble and in search of new avenues for generating profitable activity. They found their answer in a burgeoning real estate market buoyed by new tax laws that encouraged development almost irrespective of the health of the underlying economy. The savings and loans (S&Ls), flush with the excitement of the resulting runaway real estate spree and endowed with expanding lending capacity and powers courtesy of deregulation, were jumping into commercial ventures like there was no tomorrow. But there was, and we're still paying for it. Later in the decade, as tax laws changed, the economy withered, and property values inflated by rampant speculation couldn't be supported in a market with no buyers, these once-invincible growth machines were engaged in a deliberate policy of shrinking their deposit base. In the final phases of the turbulent 1980s, we were greeted with the Southwest Plan, the Resolution Trust Corporation, and the cold reality of a half-trillion dollars in lost wealth being thrust upon the taxpayers.

What is widely forgotten when people look back on this decade in Texas is the fact that it wasn't all downhill. Quite the contrary. Although we did have a recession in 1982, we also experienced a significant recovery during the ensuing few years. It has to be one of the quietest and least noticed recoveries on record, at least in retrospect. Some people don't remember it because it was uneven. It affected some parts of the state quite a bit more than others. Many of the regions closely tied to oil and gas activity did not see much of a comeback at all. In Odessa or Alice, if it wasn't happening in oil, it wasn't happening at all. Dolly Parton once sang a song called, "I'll Oil Wells Love Ya!" That's definitely the way it was in some parts of Texas.

Another reason why this "recovery" is often forgotten is the fact that much of it was driven, not by fundamental growth in export activity (such as manufacturing, agriculture, and mining), but by construction, finance, and real estate. It's hard to recognize or even imagine a recovery in which none of the traditional basic industries of the state are particularly active. A spurt of business expansion which is driven only by a secondary or spin-off activity can't hope to last for long. Building for the sake of building just doesn't work; there has to be something coming along to occupy all of that shiny new space.

The prevailing wisdom about the 1980s in Texas, often expressed by people inside and outside of the state, roughly sums things up as follows: "Well, there was this 'oil boom', see, and they built all those office buildings, shopping malls, and houses, and then they had a lot of problems and then everything went down the tubes." That synopsis is fine, except for one thing. There needed to be a long pause between the oil boom and the building of the stuff. The reality is that the frenetic real estate lending and development cycle occurred *after* the oil boom subsided. The rise of petroleum prosperity ran its course near the end of 1981; the construction frenzy didn't really crank up until 1982 and beyond. The primary role that the oil boom of the 1970s and early 1980s played in the subsequent real estate explosion was simply one of positive reinforcement, as psychologists would say. In short, it affected expectations, or what people think. Ray's Law of Economics strikes again.

The timing worked out in such a way that the incentives to develop real estate in the United States, courtesy of federal tax revisions and financial deregulation, were created at precisely the point when Texas was perceived as the best and the brightest economy going. Unfortunately, at almost exactly the same moment, the props were kicked out from under the oil industry. When that happened, the Lone Star lost its luster. Unfortunately, the sheen lingered long enough to cause a lot of foundations to be poured. These and other coincidences of the clock and the calendar would play a major role in shaping the fortunes of Texas.

By 1987, I would be describing the situation as being as rare as "the mutual alignment of nine planets." Indeed, it took a set of circumstances that could only occur once in a millenium to bring all of these forces to bear in one place at one time in such a dramatic fashion. At any rate, the generation of economic activity from construction, real estate, services, and trade does not generally give the same sense of prosperity to the "man on the street" as rigs drilling, pumps pumping, smokestacks smoking, and other signs of prosperity in traditional manufacturing and mineral industries. Such was the nature of the recovery that began in 1983. Hence, it failed to attract a great deal of fanfare.

Still another reason why many Texans and outside observers failed to notice the upswing was the fact that it did not bring back the same levels of drilling activity and related production as were observed at the height of the oil bonanza in late 1981. In the old days, rotary rig counts in the 600 to 900 range would have seemed quite prosperous. That many rigs poking holes in the ground conventionally meant that the search for new pockets of petroleum was marching right along. Yet when viewed in the wake of "boom"-era rig counts in excess of 1,400, this level of drilling activity seemed woefully inadequate.

Similarly, we shouldn't forget that oil prices during the early '80s were generally ten times higher than what we ever saw in Texas prior to the beginning of the explosion back in 1973. Nonetheless, they were well below the peak levels and were thus viewed with dismay. People's memories in economic matters tend to be terribly short; unfortunately for folks like me, who stick our necks out to prognosticate, their memories about economic forecasts tend to be much longer. I'll say more about all of these things later.

Just to give a brief perspective on the turmoil of the 1980s, let's talk about jobs. As the decade began, we Texans used that word with casual abandon, if we even bothered to talk about it at all. Jobs were a dime a dozen; we created tens of thousands of them every month. We put more than 2 million of them on the roster during the oil boom. It just sort of happened, like the rising and setting of the sun, and we didn't think much about it. We were supremely confident of continued employment expansion and success in all of our economic endeavors.

By the end of the decade, though, the "J-word" had become the pivotal guiding force for virtually every community initiative and legislative action in the entire state. It dominated all of our discussions. Repeatedly, the question of how many jobs an activity would create was the fundamental factor in the decision-making process. Just about any bill that was passed in the legislature had to have a "job quotient" attached to it. Things as disparate as economic development incentives, insurance requirements, utility regulation, tort reform, funding colleges and universities, horse racing, building transportation infrastructure, and competing for national research laboratory facilities were cloaked in the mantle of job creation and retention. Since job forecasting and impact assessment is a big part of what I do, I suppose that my group's capacity to answer that question with some degree of sophistication and accuracy in virtually any context, often under time constraints that would make your hair stand up, played a major role in our early involvement in the legislative process and in the historic events of this period.

Community efforts to build stadiums, convention centers, bridges, industrial parks, sewer systems, and reservoirs ultimately succeeded or failed on the issue of jobs. I remember during the heat of battle over the Alamodome initiative in San Antonio, proponents sported buttons, banners, and t-shirts proclaiming "DOME MEANS JOBS." As with legislative matters, our enormous set of forecasting and impact models brought me to town (just about every town) more often than not when these issues were debated. Without exception, we called 'em like we saw 'em. I recall one occasion when I was asked to attend one of those retreats people sometimes have to brainstorm ideas for their area. The leader asked me what three words first came to mind when I thought of economic development. My immediate response was "Jobs! Jobs! Jobs!" I, too, had grown to appreciate the overriding significance of the J-word in an arena where employment opportunities had been going up in puffs of smoke.

Official labor statistics showed that non-agricultural employment in Texas at the beginning of 1980 stood at slightly more than 5.7 million workers. By the end of 1981, this number jumped to about 6.3 million. In the span of less than two years, the state had seen employment spurt by 600,000 new jobs, a total increase of well over 10%. (For those of you who are keeping score, that's a gain of three Alaskas in only two years.) This growth occurred despite a very sluggish national economy, the semi-official embodiment of which was a Misery Index. There were some initial mutterings that year in the press, and probably at least a few private discussions on the ninth hole at Colonial or after dark in the Petroleum Club bar, about excess supplies of oil and a potential market glut. There was, however, little hint of what was about to ensue in Texas. Employment would peak in December of 1981. Only one year later, we had lost more than 200,000 jobs (again, one Alaska) throughout the state. The levels observed in December of 1981 would not be seen again until March of 1984. That Alaska took a little longer than some of the others.

As the state went through its recovery phase in the mid-1980s, employment moved up again, to 6.7 million people by November and December of 1985. In 1986, however, an extraordinarily severe collapse of petroleum prices again afflicted state business activity. By January of 1987, employment had fallen to 6.4 million, a loss approaching 300,000 workers (1.5 Alaskas) in only a brief 13-month period. This drop rivaled the pace at which we were adding jobs at the height of the boom. We hit bottom, jobwise, in January of 1987, although the recession in other key variables, such as income, lingered throughout most of 1987.

In early 1987, we started seeing a recovery of jobs which finally brought the state back to its previous peak by September of 1988. A little over a year later, as the dreadful decade was coming to an end, an additional 200,000 workers had been added (another Alaska). From the trough in 1987 to the end of 1989, a period of less than 3 years, we actually saw employment rise by 460,000 people, or 2.3 Alaskas.

Before your eyes glaze over with all these statistics, let me wrap this part up. We had a job peak in 1981 and a trough about a year later. Another upward spike occurred as growth continued through the end of 1985, with another trough in early 1987. A significant resurgence was observed from that point forward, although the pace was nowhere near that experienced during the boom years of the late 1970s and early 1980s. A new high was established in September of 1988, with continued employment expansion beyond that point through the remainder of the decade. In short, the 1980s in Texas will be remembered by all as a period of peaks and valleys, highs and lows, euphoria and depression. We gained and lost Alaskas like they were condos on South Padre.

While many people look back on this era in Texas with confusion and bewilderment, for someone who poured over millions of numbers, observed and participated in key events, and talked to thousands of people, the path is really quite clear. In fact, it comes back to our basic notion that the most important thing is what people think. You'll see what I mean as we expand our view and explore the details.

FIVE

The Boom Begins to Lower

1980 AND 1981

As the 1980s got underway, Texas was still moving full steam ahead. News headlines trumpeted continuing rises in oil prices and talked of a prosperous banking and real estate environment. The extraordinary began to be viewed as commonplace. Economic prosperity was almost taken for granted; it was a way of life. It seemed as if the world was totally enamored with us, and we with ourselves.

At the same time, most of the rest of the United States was again becoming mired in a severe recession. The price of oil continued to climb, and with it the fortunes of Texas. Breakthrough research announcements in the industry, such as Conoco's successful initial experimentation with horizontal drilling, strongly reinforced expectations for future production in the aging fields of Texas. (For many years, the more unscrupulous denizens of the oil patch had been known to slant the old drill bit just enough to make it over to the next guy's property. When they were caught, they had a long stint in prison ahead of them. They generally looked forward to the time behind bars. It was far more pleasant than what would be waiting for them if they even stepped foot back into the oil fields. Horizontial drilling is the ultimate, but legitimate, culmination of this concept. The latest advances would still be very much in the news as the 1980s drew to a close.)

It wasn't just oil that seemed to be rising to the top and taking Texas with it. This was also a period of mega-bank mergers and acquisitions among the large holding companies. Although the newly acquired banks couldn't be official branches at the time, the signs on the door and rapid adoption of corporate cultures sure gave the impression of a unified organizational giant. Increasingly, the directors of the smaller entities merely met, collected their modest fees, and passed whatever resolutions were sent down from the upper floors of big buildings in Dallas and Houston.

Midland, smack in the middle of the rich petroleum reserves of the Permian Basin, had become one of the most affluent places to live in the entire nation. Given its West Texas location in relative isolation from other population centers, the wealth of the area was truly startling. At one point, Midland had more Mercedes per capita than any other city in America. Every time I ventured out that way, I would find some new symbol of paradise gained. The artwork gracing the hallways, boardrooms, and offices of one of the local banks rivaled the collections in some of the country's finest museums.

Houston was universally known as "boom town." That label had traditionally been reserved for much smaller towns that suddenly saw their fortunes change for the better, usually because of the discovery of oil, gold, or some other precious commodity. Nonetheless, the Gulf Coast megalopolis certainly lived up to the moniker. Office space was so tight that some companies were falling all over themselves to sign leases as much as eighteen months in advance just so they'd have the space when they needed it. The areas of East Texas, South Texas, and West Texas that were blessed with oil reserves were also marching hurriedly along the road of economic progress. We were providing oil to a ravenous market, while becoming rig-makers and pipe-makers for the world.

At the same time, Mexico was raising its oil prices considerably, reaping the benefits of the international appetite for even its heavy Mayan crude and, in the process, generally picking itself up economically. A single stock, Tubos de Acero de Mexico S.A. (TAM), a pipe manufacturer with an exclusive monopoly contract with PeMex, the state-owned Mexican oil company, became a darling of Wall Street. Its share price went from around $1.25 to about $25 or so in the frenzy of the oil boom—a 2,000% increase.

Of course, energy stocks in general were taking off, but that one must have been launched by a sawed-off shotgun. The fact that a Mexican stock could perform so incredibly on a major U.S. exchange (the American Stock Exchange) indicates the heights of market excitement about Mexico. It may say a thing or two about analysts' reports as well. In fact, such overheated enthusiasm lured several U.S. money center banks, mostly in New York, to lend their freshly starched and ironed shirts in Mexico. Those shirts would show up later as torn, tattered, and threadbare write-offs, but that's another story.

Meanwhile, back in Texas, the beat rolled on. In December of 1980, Saudi Arabia raised the price of its benchmark light crude to $32 per barrel. Powerful Saudi Oil Minister, Sheik Yamani, boldly predicted prices of $50 per barrel by spring. Nothing seemed impossible. We thought that the sky was the limit. There was talk of $75, $80, even $100-a-barrel oil. These were not just idle rumors or wishful thinking. Such predictions were coming from the highest authorities, such as the economists from major energy companies and many top oil market experts. Even Dan Lundberg, who published what was considered the best oil pricing newsletter around at the time, was leading the choir that was singing the song of $85 in '85. The discussion was not even remotely centered around the question of whether the price would dip to $9. It was, rather, focused on when it would get to $90.

As 1981 began, the popularity of and preoccupation with Texas had reached the point that we had become a state of mind. Anything that smacked of Texas, from fashion, music, art, and food to movies, television, sports, and virtually anything else some smart marketer could cook up, dish out, or otherwise make the public swallow, was making the cash registers ring. Even cowchip jewelry became a craze. Stores sprang up all over the country that sold nothing but Texana. Basically, if it had an armadillo on it, it would sell.

In the summer of 1980, "Urban Cowboy" was the hottest thing on the silver screen. It was a toss up whether John Travolta or Gilley's mechanical bucking bull won first place in audience popularity. A couple of months later, Willie Nelson became something of a movie star, mostly playing himself in the largely autobiographical "Honeysuckle Rose."

This popularity wasn't quite universal. In some quarters of the country, we were regarded as just a little bit too arrogant about our success, a label that was at least to some extent probably justified. In the midst of the boom, there was a bumper sticker that got everybody's attention. There were several versions, but they all said something along the lines of "Drive 90 and Freeze a Yankee in the Dark." Given what was going on in other parts of the country, that attitude couldn't exactly be expected to win friends and influence people. Just about everybody forgets that the original sentiment behind "let 'em freeze in the dark" was really nothing more than a beef from Texans about the federal regulation of natural gas prices. For obvious reasons, it was interpreted by most of the rest of the world in a very different way.

I will be the first to admit that there was more than a little pro-Texas, anti-Northeast establishment bias thrown in there on the part of some of the folks who displayed the inciteful phrase on the rear of their pickup trucks. When initially conceived, however, it was a complaint about the fact that people in Texas were paying more for the natural gas that they were producing than were their counterparts on the East Coast. It's pretty safe to say, though, that a lot of the good ol' boys sporting this badge of honor on Fords and Chevys in Terlingua, Tulia, Turkey, and Timpson were only vaguely aware of the nuances of the Natural Gas Policy Act and other complex regulatory mechanisms. They just knew they were from Texas and proud of it.

It's odd looking back on it now, but that crazy bumper sticker has really established its place in history. There were plenty of other manifestations of the Texas brag, such as the countless stupid and off-color jokes about Yankees with U-Hauls, but it was that bumper sticker that kept coming back to haunt us. A few years later, the tables had turned and several members of the Texas congressional delegation were trying to conjure up interest in an oil import fee. As they sought support for this measure, they were repeatedly reminded of "let 'em freeze in the dark."

I had my own similar experiences during the latter part of the decade, while I was up in Washington trying to effect a federal solution to the thrift crisis before it reached gargantuan proportions. More often than not, I was told that there simply wasn't any interest in doing anything about it because it was a "Texas problem." I was frequently blasted with "let 'em freeze in the dark." One prominent national leader even told me of seeing a bumper sticker in Connecticut that said something like "Don't Drive at All and Put Another Texan on Welfare." I shudder to think that a misunderstood slogan could end up costing the taxpayers of this country hundreds of billions of dollars, but stranger things have happened.

As I've said before, expectations about the future were boundless. Energy experts were deeply concerned about low reserves of oil, and many were advocating that the number of domestic operating rigs be doubled. Since about one-third of all the active rigs in the country are normally working in Texas, we could obviously embrace that notion with a passion. The possibility of the exact opposite, an oil glut, which would happen just a little ways down the line, seemed remote. State revenue was projected to grow by more than 20%, largely because of anticipated funds from the oil and gas severance tax and sales tax collections in a prosperous, booming economy. The severance tax in Texas is based on both the quantity and value of extraction. Hence, even though actual production had been gradually slipping since 1972, the price was going up so much that the flow of dollars into state coffers soared.

Prosperity thus left the Texas legislature facing the happy dilemma of having to spend the excess funds available in the budget. Their biggest problem was figuring out how to spend that money fast enough. A few folks at the time were proposing a "rainy day fund," that is, an accumulated surplus in case things weren't always so good. Of course, the prevailing mood was that the economic engine would stay in high gear forever, so why worry about it. Besides, it's just about impossible to get politicians not to spend money that's already in the till (or, at least, in the revenue forecast that they are living with at the time).

As 1981 drew to a close, Texas was riding along merrily through our economic Camelot. It seemed as if the boom was as permanent as our tales about the Alamo, Goliad, and San Jacinto. Then, so slowly that hardly anybody realized it, the boom began to lower. In retrospect, there were a few rumblings about excess oil supplies in world markets. Not a glut, mind you. Just maybe some temporary glitches in the timing of demand and supply. In November of 1981, the OPEC countries agreed to a concerted effort to hold up prices, but many analysts felt it wouldn't stick. Despite these concerns, many people ignored the ominous clouds of dissent and continued to project rapid rises in oil prices over the next few years. Most Texans seemed to see nothing ahead but economic sunshine. There was a kid in Waco with a new-fangled model of some sort who was spouting off about a downturn, but he was still wet behind the ears. He was just too green to understand that this was Texas and growth was going to happen. Period.

In all seriousness, my own life was running at its usual hectic pace. I fear I have a proclivity for getting myself involved in several major projects at once. Fortunately, I have also developed a capacity for completing them all effectively. But then, I don't sleep much. Toward the end of 1981, I was crunching numbers on everything from aardvarks to zucchini as I put the finishing touches on preparations for my first forecast with the Texas model. I was also intensively involved in the final stages of the LTV security litigation. Like I say, I can't ever seem to do just one thing at a time.

In any case, I'd been developing this model for about three years and was just real proud of it. It reproduced history with uncanny accuracy. On this first attempt to use it as a forecasting tool, however, it was telling me some things about the Texas economy that didn't look so good. I kept playing with the numbers and recalculating various scenarios, hoping my model was wrong, but it didn't seem to be. I also tried to set the model aside and just look at all the numbers floating around out there with the aid of only a trained eye (or, at least, an eye in training). Unfortunately, I came away with the same basic conclusions. Boy, was I about to be in trouble!

Before I get into specifically what I saw happening that was going to hit Texas so hard, let me explain a little bit about econometric models in general, and mine in particular. I have to digress and talk about this stuff at some point. After all, I wouldn't be writing this book if I was still in the ivory tower (or concrete basement) musing over the contributions of nineteenth-century German philosophers to contemporary economic thought. I guess the eve of my first major forecast is as good a place as any.

Economic models are nothing more than mathematical attempts to describe some facet of the workings of an economy. In today's highly sophisticated and technological age, they have become pretty complex. The ones that I work with now involve about as many calculations as there are dollars in the savings and loan bailout. Living with structures of this scope and magnitude is obviously the special province of a small (and fairly weird) group of folks like myself. They are important to all of us, however, in that they form the basis for a lot of the information that we have about the economy. As you know, it's information that breeds expectations, or what people think. I've already told you on several occasions about where I stand on that one.

Let's start with a little history. I guess it's just the professor in me. Sorry. I promise, though, that this part will be pretty painless, if not exactly fascinating and engrossing. If I cared to do so, I could easily trace the origins of economic modeling to research on the human circulatory system conducted by Sir William Harvey, a British court physician in the 1600s. An even more direct link can be drawn to a French court physician, Francois Quesney, who drew fairly complex diagrams of the flows of goods and money through an economy in the 1700s. The theory on which models are based clearly predates Adam Smith's *An Inquiry into the Nature and Causes of the Wealth of Nations* (1776) and extends to encompass prominent economists even up to the present (both tall and short). For our purposes, though, let's concentrate on the folks who actually build models with real live numbers in them.

The first econometric model ever built was one for the Dutch economy developed by Jan Tinbergen, justifiably the first Nobel laureate in economics. Incidentally, he is still alive and, even in his late eighties, remains active in the discipline. He serves on the editorial board of the *International Series in Economic Modeling*, which I chair. He even contributed a chapter to our first volume a few years back. Anyway, his model was completed in 1938, and he built it, impossible as that may seem in today's computer age, with a slide rule. Obviously, it was not a real big model, less than ten equations, but it was a start. Today, models like mine contain millions of equations and who knows how many individual calculations.

Tinbergen got the ball rolling, but the person who really gave models their modern genesis—and credibility—was Lawrence Klein of the Wharton School of Business at the University of Pennsylvania. Larry started building a fairly large model of the United States in the early 1940s, and soon spread his talents to other countries as well. He's one of the pioneers in this field and now also has his own much-deserved Nobel Prize. Essentially, he called the shots on the post-War national economy. At the end of World War II, when Klein was really beginning to crank out his numbers, Keynesian economics was very much in vogue. This school of thought saw its origins in the work of the brilliant British nobleman, Sir John Manyard Keynes, whose *General Theory of Maynard Employment, Interest, and Money*, published in 1936, gave the most cogent contemporaneous explanation of the causes of (and potential cures for) the Great Depression. (I've always wondered what was so "great" about it.) His followers in some instances corrupted his original ideas so much that, shortly before his death, he would declare himself "not a Keynesian."

Keynesian economics, at least the popular version of it, basically says that you need some sort of an outside stimulus to pump up the economy. Deficit spending during a war works very nicely. As the conflict wound down, the prevailing notion was, "well, we're losing this government stimulus and, before you can say 'armistice' three times fast, we're going right back into the Depression." As we all know, it didn't exactly work out that way. Far from it. In fact, the United States enjoyed an era of rampant prosperity unprecedented in our history.

It was Larry Klein, using his newly-minted U.S. model, who first said it wasn't so. He went against prevailing "wisdom" and predicted that another depression wouldn't happen. He was seeing a lot of factors that the ruling intelligentsia missed, most notably that the pent up demand for consumer goods, generated by a wartime environment in which high-paying jobs were plentiful and the materials to make new-fangled appliances and electric gadgets were rationed, was more than enough to keep the economy perking along.

I don't know precisely how much Larry's model had to do with that prognostication, but he sure was right on target. That single prediction gave the fledgling "industry" of economic forecasting a much-needed shot of instant credibility. I really think it marks the point where the "science" of predicting the future course of the economy was born, or at least the capacity to make a living at it. (Those of us who practice this craft recognize that it is much more of an "art" than a science, but we try to keep that a secret from everyone else. Oops! Oh well, I was going to talk about it later anyway.) Larry remained very active at Wharton throughout the growth and refinement of the now world-famous Wharton model. In fact, he just retired a year or so ago. The 1950s, '60s, and '70s saw the industry blossom, as the thirst for more information grew right along with the ability of bigger computers to produce the numbers to quench it.

Let's go ahead and move back to the scene of our story, the late 1970s and early 1980s in Texas. There were lots of models of national and even global scope, the "big three" being Data Resources,

Incorporated (DRI), Chase Econometrics, and of course, Wharton. At that time, however, there was no such thing as a "homegrown" model that honed in directly and specifically on Texas. (Incidentally, Wharton and Chase have since merged and DRI is now a subsidiary of McGraw-Hill.)

The evolution of my Texas model is kind of strange. I guess several things happened at once. As I mentioned earlier, I'd been doing a lot of highly technical stuff related to Federal Reserve policy beginning with my dissertation. It was 1978, and I was busily about the task of cranking out the usual, esoteric academic articles that serve the purposes of (1) finding new and ever more creative ways to rearrange the Greek alphabet and other equally Greek symbols in largely incomprehensible combinations and (2) keeping young professors employed. I was building models of the U.S. monetary sector and teaching classes in econometrics, but not really even pondering the possibility of jumping into something of the magnitude of my current endeavors.

One bright and sunny day (actually, I don't remember what the weather was like), a student asked me if there was a model of Texas. I didn't even know, so I checked around and, best I could tell, there wasn't. The idea of building one sort of intrigued me, and some of the administrators got interested in the sense that it might bring some publicity and attention to the school. I suppose I got a little encouragement and then just started putting one together on a shoestring.

In the early days, I was fortunate enough to receive some help from the office of the Comptroller of Public Accounts (Bob Bullock). He published an article about his interest in a tax revenue model; I picked up the phone and called him to tell him about what we were doing. He ended up setting up a meeting between Bill Allaway, his forecaster at the time, and me. We worked together a little bit. He even ventured up to Waco once. Of special significance was the fact that the comptroller's office allowed me to piggyback onto some of their data base subscriptions. I wasn't exactly flush with resources, financial or otherwise, and access to this information was an enormous help to me.

Other folks in the state government were also beginning to show some curiosity. The comptroller's office, with responsibility for all state revenue forecasting, had an obvious reason to pursue economic modeling. At its best, it provides assistance in producing those vital estimates that drive the entire legislature process. At its worst, it provides a decent excuse if the predictions go awry. The governor's office expressed some curiosity as well, measured by the fact that they also brought a group to Waco. I obviously wasn't chatting with the governor at the time (the beginning of Bill Clements' first term), but the story I'm told is that he came back from some governor's conference—I have no idea which one—feeling somewhat stung by the fact that other states had models and we didn't. It was his "Texas proud" coming out. We all have it. When I started, about thirty states had models of some sort, although most were very small and many were nothing more than somebody's dissertation, just sitting on a shelf and gathering dust like most dissertations. His basic attitude was communicated to me as something like "I don't know what they are and I don't care what they do, but I want us to have one and I want it to be bigger and better than theirs!" For my own part, I really didn't know or care why the governor's office was interested. I was just grateful for the help.

A couple of other items are needed to put this whole thing in perspective. First, I was totally unaware of the fact that the University of Texas had started a model only a few months after I did. It certainly makes sense that, if the state wanted a model, they would look no further than across the street. We did not know about each other (or at least I didn't know about them) for quite awhile. By 1982, the state with no models suddenly had two of them. Given their vast resources and my meager beginnings, the story of how mine survived and theirs didn't is probably fascinating. Unfortunately, I don't know all the details and, hence, can't tell it.

The second thing to point out is that, in the late 1970s, nobody in the corporate sector saw much of a need for a sophisticated forecasting tool of this nature. After all, Texas was growing so much that they really didn't need a model or an economist to explain it to them. They could just look at the bottom line.

So what goes into these models and why do we build them? When I give my quick and dirty lecture to a class on what an econometric model is, I start with the notion that in the physical or biological sciences, you have the capacity to conduct controlled experiments. In economics, you don't. That simple fact gives rise to the need for models.

For instance, let's say, for lack of a better example, that you want to test the impact of smoking marijuana on rats. The way a scientist would go about doing that is to take two identical groups of rats into a laboratory and put them in a controlled environment. She would give them the same diet; the same amount of water; the same temperature; the same everything else, as much as possible. Then she would vary the one thing that was the subject of the experiment.

In this instance, of course, we're talking about the infamous weed; so she gives it to one group of rats and not the other, and measures the difference in various performance characteristics. I doubt if the rats could smoke a joint, so they are probably injected or something. Readings are taken on them for muscle tone, sleep patterns, endurance, and all that sort of stuff. If it is found that the rats who were given the marijuana are healthier, more verile, and have better muscle tone than the others, then it is concluded that marijuana is good for rats. Alternatively, if they are listless, sick, or dying, then the opposite conclusion is drawn. (Obviously, I haven't spent a great deal of time in a scientific laboratory, but hopefully you get the picture.)

In the economic universe, we don't have the capacity to conduct these types of experiments. Models at least let us take a decent cut at it. In other words, models exist in economics because we know so little about the world in which we function. Ideally, what you would like to do if, say, you wanted to know the impact of a different oil price on Texas is to take two identical states of Texas into a laboratory. You would then run them both ahead for five years or so under the normal external conditions, except you would change that one factor, namely the price of oil, in one of them. After you had your experiment all set up, you would simply sit there and record everything—retail sales, gross product, personal income, employment, etc. At the end of five years, you could compare your readings from the two economies and say, with some degree of scientific authority, that such-and-such was the impact of the alternative oil price conditions.

Of course, you can't do an experiment like that for a number of reasons. For one thing, in the "real world," there aren't two states of Texas, a fact which brings huge sighs of relief to people all over the East Coast. Moreover, you can't even take the one we do have into a laboratory and play with it. (I've asked several times.) You then quickly discover that there is no such thing as "normal conditions" for the economy over the next five years, nor can you even begin to hold everything else constant while you conduct your experiment. You also find out that you can't wait five years for the answer, because whoever is footing the bill wants to know yesterday!

Since you can't do it like a real scientist, the next best thing you can do is try to build a detailed and sophisticated description of how the economy works, that is, a model. You dó that by linking all the various factors together as best you can. And then with that system in place, you can do these types of exercises on a mathematical basis. You simply take a forecast from somebody else about the nation and the world for the next five years, plug it into this model that's been developed specifically for Texas, and run it out into the future. Next you change just one factor, like the price of oil, and spin it through the computer. You can then compare the results of the two exercises (or "simulations," as those of us who have been initiated call them) to see what the differences are. It's not a perfect reading, but it can give you some idea of what's going to happen.

Obviously, the more detail you put into linking things together in a model, the more information you can milk from it. Similarly, the more ways you tie it to external factors, such as oil prices, interest rates, exchange rates, and federal budgets, the more types of experiments you can conduct with it. Mine is extremely abundant on both counts. A huge piece of the Texas model is the linkage of employment, income, and output, which is all done industry by industry. With that basic core, it's possible to venture into rig counts, retail sales, housing, population, and a bunch of other stuff. In recent years, we have added impact assessments and occupations to the structure and put everything on a county-by-county basis. If you're into this stuff (and you're probably not), it's really awesome. There's definitely not another one like it.

That's enough for now. You probably now know more than you ever cared to about the life and times of economic models. I may throw in a detail or two later on, but you've endured the worst of it. Suffice it to say that there are billions of calculations involved. Like I said, I've built the model up considerably since the early days. Computers have learned to handle a lot more information, and I've picked up a thing or two along the way. But even in the early days, the model—and my gut—told me enough to foresee a bust. When they agree, they're usually right. When they disagree, I tend to go with my gut.

On that happy note, let's move back to the real world of year-end 1981. I was extremely concerned and nervous about the first set of projections I was pulling from the much ballyhooed research effort—the model that this kid, also known as me, had been putting together. In fact, my fingernails have never been so short. At this juncture, despite a little publicity (hence the ballyhoo) about the fact that there was such a model, neither it, nor I, had ventured very far out of the ivory tower and into the universe of reality, the place where all economic forecasters must ultimately prove their mettle.

It's scary enough to stick your neck out with a forecast at any point. As those of you who know me are well aware, I don't have a neck at all. I stand even at the shoulders with folks who are two or three inches taller than me. Seriously, though, it's never easy to put it all on the line, especially when you are going against a prevailing viewpoint. And back then, believe me, I was.

Worse yet, I was an unknown commodity with little access to the information required to offer a "street smart" view of business activity. Face it. I was a kid. This was to be my first forecast, and I was going to stand up and tell my fellow Texans that the boom was over. As a native, that was a real tough thing to do. But everybody has to start somewhere, and I at least had the perspective of someone who had been staring at the numbers and intensely studying the fundamental structure of the Texas economy for several years.

As I said before my intervening "lecture," something had been bothering me as I was putting together my model and getting a "feel" for the world that it sought to replicate. Something just didn't seem right about what was going on deep in the numbers of the Texas economy. My own instincts and my systematic viewing of the situation were both telling me things that ran counter to conventional wisdom. I didn't think our future looked quite so rosy.

In examining our new gross product accounts for Texas closely, I discovered that a significant segment of the much-discussed and often-touted diversification into manufacturing wasn't so diversified after all. We boasted about our thousands of new plants all the time. When viewed at an appropriately disaggregated level, however, most of our "new" manufacturing was actively tied to producing materials, pipe, and equipment to support the world oil industry. We had moved far beyond being mere drillers. Virtually every facet of our economy in the early 1980s ultimately came back to one thing. When I would occasionally sit down and try to draw a diagram of the model, it seemed like every single arrow led to another arrow that led to another arrow that led to . . . you guessed it . . . oil! We had not really diversified our economy at all; we had merely diversified (and increased) our dependence on the health of the world petroleum market. Everywhere I looked, I found oil. I should've been a wildcatter.

In the early 1980s, I certainly didn't have millions invested in wells, oil stocks, or drilling equipment (or even thousands or hundreds for that matter), but I knew that the fortunes of this wild commodity with its glorious history were a major driver of everything in Texas. Since I was about to embark on a career of forecasting in Texas, I figured I had better watch this commodity very closely. Over the years, I have picked up many nuances to help me evaluate world oil markets. I have also acquired access to people throughout the world who are experts in various parts of this crazy market, so that I can patch together a pretty complete picture of what's going on at any given time.

One nifty little trend spotter that I've picked up along the way which has served me quite well is what I call the "shiny rig" indicator. I found out in my travels, through visits to Kilgore, Alice, Odessa, and other centers of oil activity, that when contracts are in the works, rigs are usually sandblasted. I figured out real fast that if I saw shiny rigs, or rigs in the process of being shined up, I needed to get out of the car and find out what was happening. If the rigs were idle and rusting, as they were all too often in the mid-1980s, it was self-evident that nothing was happening. That forecasting tool, which we economists sometimes call a "leading indicator," works about as well as any that I've found. On a broader scale, I quickly learned the value of talking to people, traveling around, and being observant. In many cases, this kind of raw, on-the-spot research tells me as much or more than any of our technical econometric work with the numbers.

In 1981, however, numbers were all I had. And, as I just said, several of them were bothering me. In particular, I began to notice the sagging demand for oil and, at the same time, the continuing production. Although OPEC brought less oil to the market in 1981 than any time since 1969, there were other sources out there and it was apparent that the planet was beginning to gradually float on a sea of petroleum. It was even reaching the point where it was difficult to store all that was being pulled out of the ground and not consumed.

Everything spelled over-capacity to me. As best I could recall from my elementary economics courses, when there is an excess supply of a commodity in a market economy, the price falls. And when prices drop, eventually production does, too. When production no longer takes place, all of the support industries around it also suffer.

In the case of Texas, it is no exaggeration to say that, as the 1980s began, we had an economy somewhat akin to that of a company town. Oil was integrated into virtually every aspect of our business activity. The fact that there was too much of it out there gave me terrific cause for concern. Although prominent national forecasting groups that had been around a lot longer than I had were continually predicting bright things for Texas, I was worried. Moreover, my structural understanding and modeling told me that if I plugged lower oil prices into my economic system, Texas didn't fare so well.

With all of this in mind, I released my first forecast in January, 1982. It certainly didn't foresee everything that would happen in Texas, but it did predict the downturn in mining (which is over 95% oil- and gas-related in Texas) and manufacturing. It predicted difficult times in Texas during 1982, as the economy weathered the first oil glut. For years after that forecast, it seemed that no one could use my name without attributing it to me. It was always something like "Ray Perryman, *who accurately predicted the oil bust,* said this, that, or the other." Even today, almost a decade later, it still pops up fairly often.

My tendency to say exactly what I think, combined with my position as an academic in the private sector with no particular vested interest in the outcome of my projections, admittedly made a lot of folks nervous back in those days. It also helped my credibility tremendously. As I said, at first, I was very much an unknown quantity, and folks weren't so sure that I was one of the good guys (particularly when I didn't sing with the choir that said everything was going to be fine). For all they knew, I was a loose cannon. But I kept going out on the street with a forecast month after month, year after year. Because of my first one, the others got enough attention that they couldn't be ignored. After a while, people began to realize that I was the messenger, not the message. I quickly gained recognition as one who would work harder and longer than anyone else to help make things better; I just wouldn't call what I didn't see.

To be honest about it, that first forecast was a tough one to release, not so much because I worried that I wouldn't be right, but because I was scared that I was. Even if I had been completely wrong, I really didn't have much of a reputation to lose. On the other hand, you have to remember that I'm a product of a small town and grew up over in the sticks around the East Texas oil fields. It was painful for me, in late '81 and early '82, to come to grips with the fact that something bad was about to happen to Texas. I didn't realize that I was about to be placed in the middle of history, but I did know that an oil glut would have profound effects on all of us. It was difficult for me to get up and say that, not so much from an intellectual perspective, but just emotionally. It was hard for me to believe, and even harder to accept. No matter how many numbers I looked at, and how convincing they were to me, I didn't want it to happen. I'd grown up around those park benches, cafes, and domino halls in East Texas where the old oil coots hung out. Just about all anybody did over there was sit around and talk about how great Texas was. Nobody wanted to say any different, least of all me.

SIX

Maybe Things Aren't So Bad After All

THE '82 RECESSION

In 1982, Texas took a tumble. Unfortunately, the kid with the new model had been right. Why was Texas so totally unprepared for any recession and why did Texans just not think it could be that bad? There were a lot of reasons. One big thing is that good ol' optimism that we all share. We all have it, and the oil boom of the 1970s served only to reinforce it. The 1970s basically told Texans, "You're great." We didn't need a whole lot of encouragement on that front. We'd always suspected it.

I still get a kick out of some of the old "barons" over in East Texas that I personally knew or heard about who were fortunate enough to have some acreage that had oil under it. Those guys, by the time they were 60 or 70 years old and rich as all get out, began to freely advise the world on just about everything. Some of them didn't even finish the second grade, and the only thing that gave them the credentials to talk to anybody about anything is the fact that they happened to own a piece of dirt where they poked a hole and found black gold. Nevertheless, they would spout wisdom to the world, and in the process, give their philosophy about what made them, and Texas, so successful. The funny thing about it is the fact that we have always listened to them and taken heed.

In reality, of course, Texas was a resource-based economy and our "success" was the result of luck as much as anything else. Yet the pearls from the lips of people with the trappings of the incomprehensible wealth that oil can bring helped us to pretty much convince ourselves that we were doing better than the rest of the country, not because we had oil, but because we worked hard and were just so much brighter than everyone else. (One interesting sidelight to the random nature in which Texans became filthy rich is an amazing preoccupation, to the point of obsession, with the mineral rights attached to property. We don't quibble about price per acre all that much, and we're perfectly satisfied with a surveyor's report that says "120 acres, more or less." While the metes and bounds don't bother us, we get real particular about those mineral rights. A misunderstanding on that issue, even over a small residential lot, will bring the guns to the table.)

The other thing you have to remember about the early 1980s is that we are not only talking about our usual preaching to the choir. We admittedly do a lot of that, but all the itinerant ministers from other places were also delivering the same message. It seemed that just about everybody outside of Texas was thinking, believing, and telling us we were good, too. Texas was hot! The art, the music, the cuisine. Even our football teams were winning! I mean everything was right with the world—our world, that is—and every possible positive thing seemed to be coming our way. I can try to communicate it, but it was the kind of an environment where you almost had to be there to understand the collective mood. We could do no wrong, and people just kind of got caught up in it.

At the height of the celebration of all things Texan, our economic fortunes were turning downward. We didn't want to admit it, but the unthinkable, a Texas recession, was happening. As I mentioned earlier, nonagricultural employment reached a peak in the state at the end of 1981 and continued to decline until early 1983. Of even more interest, however, were some of the underlying numbers. Manufacturing employment topped out in September of 1981, at levels which haven't yet been reestablished.

We hit the real bottom in manufacturing employment at the beginning of 1987, with more than 200,000 jobs in this highly paid export sector being eliminated. (That equals, you got it, one Alaska.) Mineral extraction, which means oil workers mostly, reached an employment peak in January of 1982. There were over 324,000 workers of various sorts out in the oil fields or in related occupations. Suddenly, the oil glut was upon us, as both price and demand hit the skids. Within the next several years, we would hit a low of 173,500 mining workers. That's almost a 50% overall drop. It's doubtful that we will again see 300,000 of our finest drilling for oil anytime soon—no matter what happens in the Persian Gulf.

A look at the rig count numbers within the state will give an even more dramatic picture. As noted before, many folks in Texas think that the sun rises and sets on this single number. Tell them how many drill bits are boring holes in Texas soil, and they'll tell you how we're doing. If you were to rely only on the historical record, this system wouldn't be half bad. When you go a little further out in time, however, you'll begin to discover that a lot of other things matter. In December of 1981, Texans were drilling away as fast as they could get the rigs up and running. We had an all time high of almost 1,450 operating rigs throughout the state, the single highest month since records have been actively maintained.

Even Exxon, the most conservative of the major oil companies throughout the oil boom, decided in May of 1981 that it was finally time to throw caution to the winds and significantly increase its drilling and exploration budget across the board. The last time we'd ever seen anything close to this peak in activity was at the end of 1951, when demand was generated by a surging peacetime economy and the escalating energy needs of the Korean conflict. We had emerged from World War II as the only major industrial country in the entire Free World with its productive capacity fully intact, and were just beginning that marvelous era of global dominance. (To put all that in my perspective, I wouldn't even be born until near the end of 1952.)

Rig counts almost invariably spike at the end of the year, often in the middle of some pretty treacherous weather. That fact simply demonstrates that the Internal Revenue Service can at times define seasonality better than the National Weather Service. Getting a well underway at the end of the year can offer some serious tax advantages. With the tax laws of the early 1980s, it really paid off to crank one up in December.

In 1982, the rig count began to drop. By June of 1983, it was down to 687 operating platforms, or less than half the peak of only eighteen months earlier. In fact, that was the first trough in the drilling cycle of the early 1980s. It was largely forgotten that the 687 rigs in service at the time represented more activity than any level achieved between 1960 and the latter part of 1975. In other words, our "lows" during this initial drilling slump were higher than our "highs" in much of the history of drilling in the state prior to the great oil boom. As I've said before, people's memories on economic matters are excruciatingly short. A rig count below 700 was viewed as evidence of a tremendous slump. Folks in Texas may not put much stock in any other numbers, but they do sit up and take notice when the rigs stop running. (Today, the oil patch bunch would give their eye teeth to see 687 rigs on the line.)

The count would briefly rise above 900 again in 1983 and 1984, achieving levels above anything seen at any point in the 1960s or the 1970s. When it started falling again, it would begin a downward slide (or outright free fall) that would carry it all the way to a low of only 216 operating rigs. That paltry number represented the lowest point in the entire period for which records have been consistently maintained. It shows us just how far down the industry can go when demand sags, prices fall, OPEC cheats, and Congress strips away some of those wonderful tax goodies.

Now, as I've said, my initial forecast in January 1982, called some of this imminent fiasco. Oil, to which our general fortunes were so closely tied, was going to let us down . . . and not so gently. But many were ignoring the signs, refusing to believe what was rapidly becoming the obvious. As I've said before, the most important thing is what people think. Our bankers, legislators, and business leaders did not think anything very bad was going to happen, so they didn't plan or act accordingly. Basically, there was just this general notion that Texas couldn't have a recession. I started getting a real sense of that when I gave the first four or five speeches to bankers and other industry groups around the state after my forecast was released. Nowadays, folks call months in advance to get on my calendar. Back then, I was the new kid on the block, and I'd talk just about anytime to just about anybody that would let me. I was out there saying, "Hey, we're in a recession." The response was almost universally, "Oh, no. You can't be right! You're mistaken! You better go check all those fancy numbers and formulas again. Son, you're in Texas!" Attitudes have changed considerably over the years.

People often ask me today about how I felt at the time. I mean, I was one of the first people to see that the storm was about to hit the coast. (Y'all know what I really mean.) Was I scared? Did I sell off my stock?

First off, I didn't have any money to buy stock at the time, so that wasn't an issue. Was I scared? Probably. The real frustration for me at the time was that I was out there saying, "It's happening, just as sure as I'm short." That wasn't easy for me, and the fact that nobody paid much attention to me made it doubly difficult. It's pretty ironic, really. Today, a casual remark to a friend at a party or an off-the-cuff answer to a question at a speech or press conference can find its way into several hundred newspapers by the next morning. My mouth gets me in trouble all the time. My friends and colleagues tell me that they are constantly bombarded by people asking, "What does Ray have to say about this or that?" In 1982, though, I was little more than a voice crying in the wilderness.

Looking back on it now, I can certainly understand why I wasn't taken too seriously. In fact, I can even go so far as to say that, if I had been in the boots of the business and financial leaders of Texas at the time, I would have probably responded the same way. If some kid who had never done this stuff before came out of nowhere today and gave a forecast that was totally different from the conventional wisdom, I might well ignore it, too. It was kind of like the old stories of Nero fiddling while Rome burned or the band continuing to play as the Titanic began to sink. Not only did the music continue to be heard, but the folks in charge really didn't even know—or want to know—that the embers were ablaze and the ship was taking on water.

Was I angry that no one was listening? No, not really. I don't tend to get angry very often (unless, of course, you interfere with lunch). I think I was more frustrated than anything else. That's the feeling that sticks in my mind. After my forecast had been out there for about four months, the University of Texas group came out with their first forecast. It was considerably more optimistic than mine.

Once that one came out, it was really tough to get my message across. People kept saying, "Well, son, you understand now that you're not from the University of Texas; you don't know what's happening. It's as plain as the nose on your face that you don't know what's going on. They've just told us everything is going to be wonderful. You just haven't been out in the field long enough to know what we know about Texas." I certainly couldn't argue with the last part of that sentiment. On the other hand, I had not (and still have not) ever seen so many numbers line up the same way.

I had really expended my energies trying to get people to listen to that forecast, hoping that it could help us to minimize or at least cope with the damage. Unfortunately, it wasn't until later that folks began to take me seriously. But, in a sense, my first forecast did for me what Larry Klein's post-World War II call did for him and the entire discipline; it gave credibility to my model and to me.

After about the midpoint of 1982, the media began to make noises about some recessionary signs in Texas. Indeed, there were enough casualties along the way that year to make a goodly number of people sit up and take notice. (It was hard for me to notice much of anything economic in the middle of 1982; my first daughter, Skye Lynn, was born on June 9.) By the end of that fateful twelve months, everybody pretty much had to come to grips with the fact that the impossible had indeed happened.

The basic ailment, of course, was oil-related. The drilling industry, which had been surging forward at impressive rates in 1981, was felled by a worldwide petroleum glut. This disease proved to be quite contagious, and heaped serious afflictions on leading manufacturing industries within the state, including oil field equipment producers, steel mills that churned out pipe by the mile, and even refining and petrochemical facilities. You would think that the petrochemical plants that use oil as an input would love to have cheaper prices. A few years down the road, there would indeed be a spurt of new investment in this sector. The immediate reaction, however, was pretty much cutbacks across the board. You have to remember that (1) oil demand was sagging and (2) the people who owned most of the refining and petrochemical facilities also owned the wells. On the whole, they were just plain scared. It took awhile to figure out what was good and what was bad; they knew that it was all ugly.

The side effects of the sickness in the oil industry were also felt by financial institutions that were leveraged to the top of the star on the San Jacinto Monument in loans to people in the oil patch. Some of the banks had also been doling out funds pretty heavily in Mexico. After all, they were our neighbors, the Feds were encouraging it, and, besides, they had all of that oil under the ground that would make debt service and retirement a snap. Yeah! Right! The peso started plummeting and the solvency of the entire country was suddenly in jeopardy. This basic currency unit of Mexico was in the process of falling from a value of 8¢ to only a miniscule fraction of a penny. This situation also didn't exactly do wonders for retail sales along the border. Another group not immune to the germs was our fearless leaders in Austin. State spending had been set in an environment which anticipated a much more robust energy market (and Texas economy).

By the end of 1982, it was pretty clear that our patient had been pretty ill. As luck would have it, we also went through a modest setback in the electronics industry at about the same time. Everybody would be real excited a few months later about the fact that a highly publicized computer research consortion, known as Microelectronics and Computer Technology Corporation spurned scores of other offers in deciding to make a home in Austin's "silicon gulch." At the moment, however, the world pretty much had its fill of semiconductors and chips. All things considered, our disease was turning into something of an epidemic.

A couple of news items during the year will give a few additional readings from the patient's medical chart, at least as far as symptoms go. On February 17, 1982, domestic crude prices dropped to their lowest level in two and a half years. During the following month, gasoline prices nationwide suffered their most precipitous drop in history. By early spring, it had become clear that the Texas hospitality industry had been injured severely, as a near lethal combination of the widespread recession, the Mexican peso collapse, and a general room glut just about pulled the shades on Texas' hotel business. Its condition was critical, though not quite terminal.

In September, bankruptcy numbers were published which indicated that a total of seventeen Dallas area oil companies had gone under in the first half of 1982, almost triple the rate of the year before. The unemployment rate in Texas topped 8% in October, the highest level in state history. We would shatter that record a couple of additional times in this initial recession of the 1980s, with the jobless figure reaching 8.8% in early 1983.

Some of the more interesting phenomena of the recession in 1982 were not the numbers that fell, but those that suffered little or even prospered. Construction employment remained remarkably healthy, as did that in the finance, insurance, and real estate sector. The commercial and residential development numbers zoomed upward; both Houston and Dallas were among the nation's leaders in bringing new space to the market. In fact, Houston remained the leading office market in the country, and there was a shortage of space in downtown Dallas. New plans for major projects were announced in Texas almost faster than architects could draw up the blueprints.

There was at least some justification for this phenomenon. Although the oil market was tumbling, the peso was falling, and we were facing a fiscal crisis, out-of-staters continued to move into Texas in droves, and we continued to create space to accommodate them. Unfortunately, because of what people think, we also built enough houses, offices, and stores to accommodate all the folks that we assumed would move here, but never did. We even did the neighborly thing and put together a little extra for the folks that had no intention of moving here. You never know when they might change their minds.

Like everything else in Texas, when we decided to build some space—son, we built some space! It was another one of those cases where you just had to be there. At one point, there was more square footage under construction in downtown Austin than there was existing office space. When you stop and think about it, just about the only people who rent offices next door to the state capitol are lobbyists, political consultants, and lawyers. Surely, we don't need twice as many of those folks. No matter how many humongous high-tech heirarchies end up in Austin, they can't be expected to sign too many leases along Congress or Guadalupe (unless, like me, they have a serious affinity for the fresh homemade candy at the Uptown Enchilada Bar over on Lavaca).

I don't want to dwell on them, but let me throw out a few numbers just to give you a picture of what was going on. In 1980, Texas had added about 126,000 units to its housing stock; in 1981, the total for the year rose to 135,000. These new residential permits represented a robust and improving real estate market in the midst of an economic boom, and should come as no big surprise. The irony, however, comes from what happened next. Believe it or not, during the recessionary year of 1982, the number of new permits rose to almost 200,000. Incredibly, there were even more in 1983, when a record total of more than 271,000 new housing permits were issued. In 1984, there were 193,000 additional units added, with another 142,000 coming on line in 1985. If you add all of that up, it comes to more than 800,000 units in only four years. That's more than we built during the entire oil boom, yet we did it during the early days of the oil bust. Anybody who lived in "old" Dallas or Houston at the time can tell you about the housing developments and apartment complexes sprouting like mushrooms out of land where cattle had grazed only a few months earlier. It all seemed to happen practically overnight.

What those numbers tell you, in retrospect, is that building activity in the residential market (and every other real estate market, for that matter) in Texas during our "recession" and sluggish period for petroleum prices far exceeded that which occurred during the more prosperous era in which oil and gas activity peaked. And guess who was financing all those hammers, nails, and I-beams? Indeed, it was the banks, thrifts (S&Ls), and every other kind of financial institution that you can name. Some of them were seeking to diversify away from oil, so they moved into real estate (it was something about a frying pan and a fire). Others were flexing the muscles recently bestowed on them by financial deregulation. It makes sense that, without oil providing the much-needed shot-in-the arm, we wouldn't be able to make the stuff to create the jobs to bring in the people to go to the realtors to sign the papers to take to the banks to get the money to buy the houses that Jack built. But never mind that; Jack, and all of his brothers, sisters, and cousins, continued to build them anyway. Hindsight is really wonderful.

Once that building "boom" started down, it really tumbled like a house of cards (pardon another pun). By 1987, there were only 50,000 housing permits issued, and even fewer in 1988 and 1989. In other words, during the final three years of the 1980s, the number of new housing permits was less than *half* of the total issued in 1983 alone. In some of the oil towns, it got so bad that they stopped numbering building permits and started naming them.

Why in the world did a building boom begin at precisely the moment that a major recession occurred? The answer lies in several basic factors that managed to come together at a single point in time and space. They all ultimately come down to my simple premise that the most important thing is what people think.

One reason for the seeming contradiction of an exploding real estate frenzy and an imploding economy is the fact that there is usually a lag between what's actually going on in an economy and what people think. For most of the country, as I've said, Texas remained the symbol of prosperity as 1982 dawned, despite some vital signs to the contrary. Only a few very well-informed people were aware that our key export industries had already topped out and were, in fact, in a slump. Even among those who were cognizant of the situation, most didn't seem to think we had a serious or permanent problem. We just sort of reckoned that we would figure something out. After all, this is Texas. Adding fuel to the fires of positive thought, a lot of people in positions to be listened to were still predicting, or wanting to believe the possibility, that oil prices would soar again in the mid to late 1980s. Certainly, to those people who had been laid off from the steel mills and automobile plants in the Rust Belt, Texas was viewed as Mecca with a capital "M" for Money. "Dallas" was still topping the ratings, the Ewings were making big bucks, and the talk around the dinner table hadn't gotten around to the latest OPEC discord. Folks came in by the U-Haul load, only to find upon arrival that things weren't exactly like what they saw on television.

At about the same time, everybody got all excited about "high tech." *Megatrends,* John Naisbitt's popular epistle, stirred the waters, naming both Austin and San Antonio as cities of the future. In May of 1983, as I mentioned earlier, Austin was selected as the site of Microelectronics and Computer Technology Corporation, which was considered a major coup. This research facility, in and of itself, was not ever intended to be a major economic generator. As a consortium of talent from various major electronic component manufacturers from around the country, it was expected to be conducting fairly esoteric research on fifth generation computer technology (machines that think). Symbolically, however, the selection of our state for such a futuristic research facility was extremely critical. It sent a message to the world that Texas was definitely stepping up to the plate in the high technology game. Ironically, because it came in the middle of the single biggest building year in the entire history of the state, the attendant publicity may have contributed to the real estate frenzy far more than we realized. The prevailing attitude at the time was that Texas had oil, and it was still going to $85 a barrel (or at least $65 or $70); now, the state was going to get a good chunk of that high tech stuff, too.

The MCC announcement raised the profile of the Austin/San Antonio region considerably, while it also increased the national visibility and political clout of San Antonio's mayor, Henry Cisneros. His vision and efforts to forge a San Antonio/Austin regional alliance clearly helped to clinch the MCC deal. The MCC announcement also helped Austin and the whole region to solidify a position as a significant center for a major growth industry. Many subsequent locations and expansions in the area, most notably the Sematech electronics manufacturing consortium, a large 3M facility, and the Bell Computer operation, have been positively influenced by the presence of MCC. Nonetheless, its initial overall impact was far greater in terms of how it affected what people think. We were now undeniably a key player in the high tech derby. Back in those days, nobody understood much about what these industries were, or, more important, what they weren't. (I wouldn't give that speech until a year or so later!) Everybody was totally enamored with the technology companies, as they seemed to the casual observer to offer an immediate panacea to our economic woes. We tried to convince ourselves that the answer to all of our problems was as easy as "Goodbye rigs and hello chips!" That would be nice!

While the lag in figuring out what was happening and the magnificent obsession with all things technological both had their place in explaining the real estate debacle, the real story lies in the changes in federal fiscal and regulatory policies. ("Debacle" is a fairly unusual word that I use a lot. I won the spelling bee with it in the seventh grade; after that, it just stayed around in my brain.) The enactment of the Reagan tax cut, also known as the Gramm-Latta bill (that's right, our own Senator, then Representative, Phil), was a big piece of the puzzle. The bill was touted publicly and best known at the time for significantly lowering personal tax rates over a period of several years. Folks were talking about "supply-side" economics and how we could cut taxes and grow our way out of the mounting budget deficits. For reasons that I never quite understood, this "supply-side" theory was implemented with a huge "demand-side" stimulus. In essence, we put more spending money in people's hands. The result was predictable. The nation started growing like gangbusters. (Lower oil prices also didn't hurt the situation any.) We took off on the longest expansion in history, but so did the deficit. It's several times as large now as it was back then.

Although the initial splash and dash was all about lower tax rates, the ultimate legacy of this legislation lies in some of the fine print. While somewhat obscure at the time, certain provisions of this law had the effect of flashing a huge neon sign that said "Build Real Estate!" This measure reduced the write-off period for real estate to only seventeen years and allowed accelerated recovery of these investments. It also retained all of the old capital gains provisions. All of this technical jargon basically says, "Don't ask questions, just build stuff!" Anybody who had the wherewithal and didn't think about getting into the real estate game was considered to be at least one brick short of a load. Practically every brokerage firm, analyst, and tax advisor in the country was putting clients into these ventures.

At the same time that all this cozy tax incentive stuff was going into effect, there was also the movement toward federal deregulation of financial institutions. Before all was said and done, virtually all banks, thrifts, insurance companies, brokerage firms, and folks with $5 and a station wagon were in a position to be real estate lenders. This new structure was ideal for Texas banks to jump into, as they were looking for a place to put their money that didn't have a derrick on top of it. To make the situation even more explosive, regulation was not uniform across institutions. In fact, the thrifts were actually in a position to become direct partners in real estate investments. It was something akin to a fox guarding a hen house.

I am a big fan of deregulation in principal. It has been my experience that free and unfettered markets generally work fairly well. In fact, another major event during 1982 that would change all of our lives had to do with the ultimate deregulation of the telephone system. In August of 1982, the fact that the breakup of AT&T was actually going to happen became official. By the end of the decade, I would find myself testifying on the proper role of regulation as a substitute for competition in telecommunications services and as a means to encourage economic development and incentives for future investment.

In the case of the financial institutions in Texas, and elsewhere for that matter, I think it is now readily apparent even to the folks in the nickel seats that the deregulation process did not create sufficient safeguards for real estate lending. People with absolutely no experience in this arena were suddenly thrust into "opportunities" that would strain the expertise of even the most experienced lending officer. The situation was essentially driven by new tax incentives and wholesale deregulation. Add to that the intense desire of Texas bankers to scoot away from energy. Maybe stir in a little greed or inexperience or both, here and there. Just for good measure, throw in the global perception that Texas is recession-proof and a great place to invest hot dollars. All of a sudden, you have yourself a situation in which real estate development becomes the order of the day. What you end up with is a building boom the likes of which Texas has never seen. Dollars, timber, concrete, glass, and steel come roaring in like a hurricane on the Gulf Coast. At the exact moment when all of this stuff gets together, if you then kick the props out from under the basic economy, you have the makings of a real disaster.

Such would be the 1980s, but we didn't know it as we poured those innumerable foundations for those magnificent edifices that would alter our landscape forever. The changes we would see over the next few years were totally beyond belief. In June of 1981, less than a year before the oil glut hit us, there was a highly publicized merger between First International Bancshares and Austin Bancshares, as they pooled assets to become bigger and make larger and more aggressive loans. It was by far the most ambitious bank merger in Texas history to that point in time, and the regulators put some close eyeballs on it. As the seeds being planted in the early 1980s were harvested later in the decade, this transaction would fade into distant memory and pale into oblivion, much like the flea on the ear of a much bigger beast.

In countless speeches that I've given to all types of groups throughout the country, I have acted out a little dramatic dialogue that probably tells as much about the origin of our financial and real estate problems as all the textbooks in the Harvard Business School. The scene takes place in 1982. I've just received a prospectus about a real estate limited partnership and the broker is following up with a phone call. This particular venture, like so many others, is composed primarily of properties scattered across Texas, with a few outside the state thrown in for good measure. Once the pleasantries are exchanged (Texans are always polite; it's what our mamas teach us), the conversation between me and the eager broker goes something like this:

"Now, let me get this straight. I want to make real sure I understand everything. You want me to give you $10,000 to put in this di-ver-si-fied port-fo-li-o?" (I say that one in a very exaggerated drawl, Texas style!).

"That's right."

"Well, I'm from the country, and that's a lot of money. Just what do I get for my $10,000?"

"Well," says the fast talking broker, "we'll take your $10,000 and borrow $90,000 from a bank and buy you a $100,000 share of this real estate portfolio. It's something we call leverage, but you don't need to worry about the details. You'll own a little piece of this, a small chunk of that, and a decent hunk of the other. That's what I mean by diversifying."

I scratch my head and say, "Now wait a minute, I didn't just fall off that turnip truck. If this real estate deal doesn't work, won't I owe a bank somewhere $90,000? That's a little deep for this poor boy's pockets!"

"Oh, no! Not at all! This is what we call a non-recourse note. You are only risking the $10,000 that you invest."

"Now, wait just a minute. Hold on there. You're saying that I put in $10,000, the bank puts in $90,000, and if things go bad, I don't have to pay back the money?"

"That's right."

"What kind of bank would be silly enough to make a loan like that?"

"All of them. Man, they're lining up to do it since that new bill was passed."

"Well, I'm still interested, so keep talking to me."

"Well, you'll get some tax advantages from this transaction."

"Look here; I'm in a 50% tax bracket, so I could sure use some help on my taxes [I'm lying here, you understand, particularly as things were in the early 1980s, but for the sake of demonstration, it does make arithmetic a little easier.] Tell me about these tax breaks."

"Well, you can write off about 40% of this investment over the first few years."

"40%?"

"That's right."

"Of 100,000?"

"Yeah."

"That's $40,000."

"You got it."

"If I'm in a 50% tax bracket, that means I save $20,000."

"That's right."

"Man, I only put in $10,000!"

"That's right."

"Now I'm slow, so let me go over this one more time. I put in $10,000, the bank puts in $90,000, and they take the risk on their part of it. I get myself a piece of this di-ver-si-fied port-fo-li-o, then the government gives me $20,000, and I still have the stuff."

"That's right."

"I'm still listening; keep talking!"

"Well, we'll manage this property for you for a few years, and then we'll sell it. You know the way things have been going lately, real estate triples about every five years." (He nods his head real forcefully on that one, so I let him keep talking.) "The bottom line to of all of this, Ray, is that after you pay back the bank, pay our fees, and have a little bit of depreciation recapture (another one of those technical things you don't need to worry about), you'll end up with well over $100,000 after taxes."

"After taxes?"

"That's right. You see, this is what the government calls a long-term capital gain and they can only take 20% of your profits."

"So I keep over $100,000?"

"That's right."

"But, . . . I only put in $10,000!"

"You're catching on, kid."

"You're gonna have to forgive me, man, but I'm from the country and I'm slow. I'm gonna have to go over this thing one more time. I put in $10,000; the bank puts in $90,000, and they take the risk. Then the government gives me $20,000 and, a few years later, you give me $100,000. Now is that the deal?"

"Yeah, if everything works out O.K., that's the deal."

"Sold!!"

Hard as it may be to swallow that little bit of dialogue now, especially with a straight face, it tells an awful lot about how we ended up in this mess. That story has been good for thousands of laughs, but it also brought its share of knowing, telling smiles and even a few outright grimaces. I had one poor fellow in Amarillo come up to me one day and say that he even borrowed the first $10,000.

In essence, an environment was created that was highly conducive to excessive real estate investment. It was a system that was ripe for abuse and one which I would spend a great deal of my time during the latter part of the 1980s (and on into the 1990s) helping to clean up.

Several years later, I finally figured out that a "di-ver-si-fied port-fo-li-o" was little more than empty apartments in North

Houston, South Houston, East Houston, and West Houston. Admittedly, I fractured a few of the fine points of the tax code in telling that story, but it does give an accurate description of the go-go environment and the cavalier attitude that prevailed at the time.

We had a new tax and financing climate that encouraged this sort of thing. We had a state that was viewed as the prime area of prosperity in virtually the entire free world. At the same time, many of the cities of the "Rust Belt" appeared to be inevitable victims of a period of long, slow decline. Yet Texas would continue to grow, or so it appeared. In fact, the only place that initially experienced the same degree of over-heated overdevelopment as the major urban areas of Texas was Denver. The reasons were exactly the same. Denver was also an oil center that received a good deal of positive attention and publicity. Texas had "Dallas," while Denver had "Dynasty." As the world finally realized that our regional economy had fallen on hard times and, simultaneously, other parts of the country began to improve, the tidal waves of new development shifted to other parts of the country (and many are now trying to keep from drowning).

The honors for "first and worst, where the bubble did burst," clearly belong to the Lone Star State. We had the initial real estate spurt to surface from the new legal environment and, a few years later, the first taste of the tragedy of excess. The rest of the nation would ultimately feel the pain, but most places were perking along rather nicely at the time.

But when we boomed, oh how we boomed! Through an amazing confluence of circumstances, we managed to set all time records in building while the underlying fabric of our basic economy was being stripped away. In 1982, Texas had six bank failures, more than one-third of the total in the entire country. At the time, nobody's crystal ball could have foreseen that oil prices would take a riveting turn downward in the middle of the decade, plunging all the way to a piddling $9 a barrel. Little did we know that the bank failures of 1982 were only a sneak preview of the financial disintegration that would ultimately take place.

Texas learned many things during this period of time. As we weathered the 1982 downturn, one thing that we finally came to realize was that we were indeed experiencing fundamental structural changes that could neither be ignored nor resolved in a short period of time. When the glut started, the immediate attitude was that it didn't matter. We would grow anyway. Then, we said it was only temporary. When we got past that one, we decided that, if we threw enough money at it and waited a while, everything would be fine. We'd been fixing things in Texas with that formula for years. Much like the phases one goes through in accepting the death of a loved one, we had to endure an arduous journey in coping with the death of one type of economy and the birth of another.

Even in the midst of 1982, however, we managed to find those wonderful bright spots that keep our frontier spirit alive and well. In September, Ross Perot, Jr., began a daredevil helicopter trip around the world, in a machine known as the "Spirit of Texas." This successful voyage, the first of its kind, was a major accomplishment in the annals of aviation. The "Spirit" and an accompanying film are now on exhibit at the Smithsonian's Air and Space Museum. It is also a testimonial to the sense of adventure and achievement that seems to be perpetuated in this state. During that same year, the extravagant Galleria Shopping Center opened in North Dallas, rivaling her sister center in Houston. Not to be outdone, the oil crowd also had its moment. The annual Oil Show in Houston drew a record crowd, despite the downturn in the industry. It seems that, in typical wildcatting style, everyone shared a great deal of enthusiasm at the meeting and that the general feeling was that the worst was behind them.

By the end of 1982, it was obvious that the unbelievable had happened. Texas, considered only a few months earlier to be invulnerable, had indeed experienced a significant recession. It contained job losses, output declines, problems in the financial sector, and all of the other classic signs of a business downturn. But by the end of 1982, it looked as if we were turning around and that the worst might be over. At least, the next few years were looking better. Although oil was sluggish, real estate was really beginning to take off. We were already developing and fine tuning our bravado. We talked about how adversity had tested us, and how we had proved our mettle. We had shown the world that we could take it with the best of 'em and still come back. Maybe it hadn't been so bad after all. Yeah! Right!

SEVEN

Recovery, But No Longer Wild And Free

1983–85

The recession in 1982 turned out to be quite a shocker. Texas hadn't seen anything like that in a long, long time. It wasn't supposed to happen. It might have even humbled us some, but not much. We lost jobs, money, businesses, and all of the other things that you lose at a time like that. In 1983, 1984, and even through most of 1985, we had a nice little turnaround. In many ways, these are the forgotten years of the 1980s. Although we talked quite a bit about it at the time, a lot of people in Texas simply don't seem to recall that there were really two recessions—the one in 1982 and another, much more severe one in 1986.

As I said in my earlier synopsis of the 1980s, we forget the first comeback because it was uneven; the folks in the oil patch didn't see much of a recovery. We forget it because it wasn't quite a Texas-style boom. Oil just kind of sat there and didn't do much of anything. A lot of Texans, particularly at that time, just couldn't imagine a recovery where the wells weren't pumping and the rigs weren't working day and night. We also forget our comeback because its genesis and its strength were in banking, finance, and real estate. Those industries are supposed to follow, not lead.

I think there is something of a tendency to rewrite history to suit our current world view. In fact, Thomas Kuhn, the eminent scientific philosopher, talks about this very phenomenon in his classic *Structure of Scientific Revolutions*, a book that permanently altered the way we think about our universe (whether or not we're consciously aware of it). He says that when new theories are developed, one of the first things we do is go out and rewrite all the textbooks. We have to make sure everybody sings from the same hymnal. Given what happened to us as the 1980s unfolded, we would like to say that the real estate boom was a part of the oil boom; that it was just another phase of the celebration of an ecstatic economic era. That would be a whole lot easier to take, and plenty of folks have tried to recast history in those terms. It's hard to admit that we had a strong recovery that was based almost entirely on building stuff when there wasn't much underlying industrial growth to occupy, let alone pay for, the space. You can't just make boxes, without ever making anything to go in them. If you look at the record and read the numbers, though, that's exactly what happened. We may as well tell it like it is.

The fact that a significant resurgence occurred in the 1983-1985 period certainly can't be denied. A quick look at some simple statistics will tell you that. By the first quarter of 1984, the previous heights in employment had again been reached. Before this recovery ran its course, more than 300,000 additional jobs would be added to the economy (1.5 Alaskas). In fact, from the employment trough in early 1983 to the peak in late 1985, the Texas economy gained almost 600,000 jobs, or three Alaskas. (By the way, I'm not the only Texan to measure things relative to other states. Out in West Texas, the standard unit of account for large ranches is not acres or sections, but "RIs." For the uninitiated, one RI is equivalent to the amount of land found within the geographic boundaries of Rhode Island.)

One of the things that enabled the economy to hold its own initially, ironically, was oil. The petroleum industry wasn't growing, but at least it wasn't plunging. Oil prices stabilized remarkably. Early in 1983, the producers in the North Sea lowered prices by about $5 per barrel, but in March of that year, OPEC developed a new benchmark price of $29 per barrel and stuck with it (a fact which greatly relieved Texas bankers, drillers, and just plain folks). By June, the price had reasonably settled in at that level, and most analysts were projecting that the slide was over. Prices

When Texas fought for independence at the Alamo in 1836,
Cattle was our dominant industry.

Photos courtesy: The Texas Collection, Baylor University

Worswick-Haard Cotton Harvester (Montgomery, Alabama invention) demonstrated on L.B. Daughtery farm in Waco, Texas in September, 1911.

"Cotton is King"

Men of Yancey, Texas who worked at one of three cotton gins in the early 1900s.

Photos courtesy, The Texas Collection, Baylor University

Photo courtesy: The Texas Collection, Baylor University

Spindletop 1901. A new industry is born.

The upside down "V"s' tell it all.

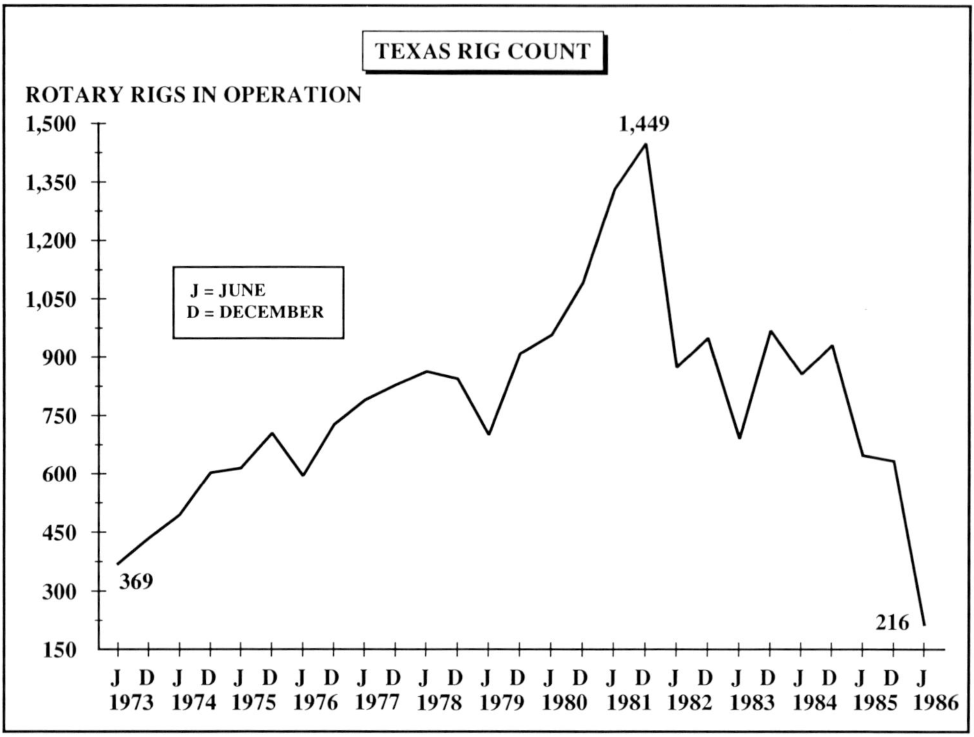

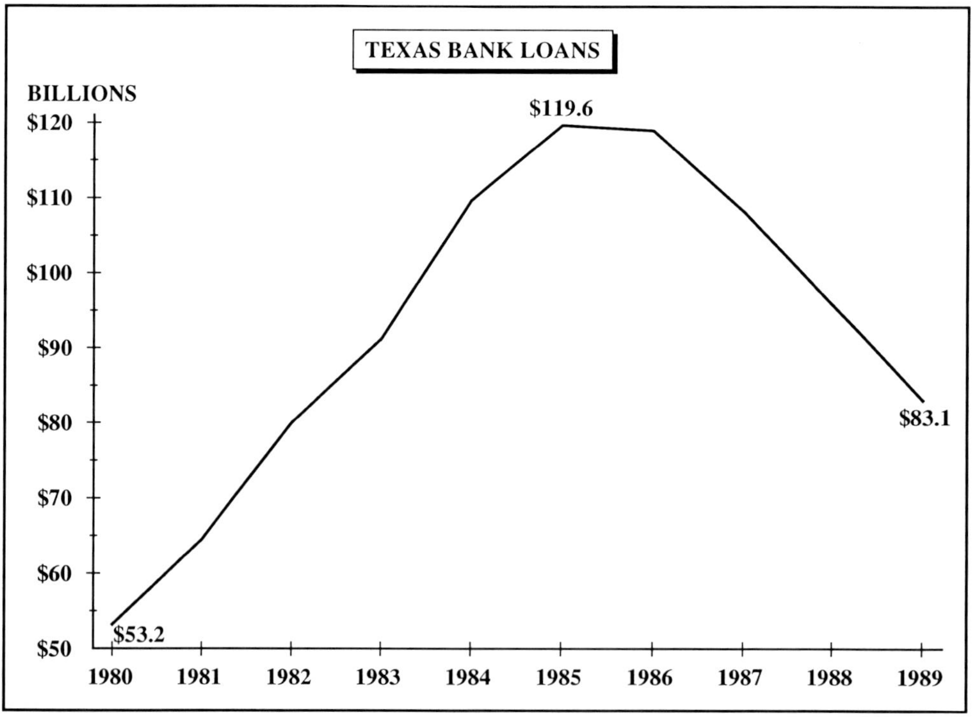

Graphs courtesy: Perryman Consultants, Inc.

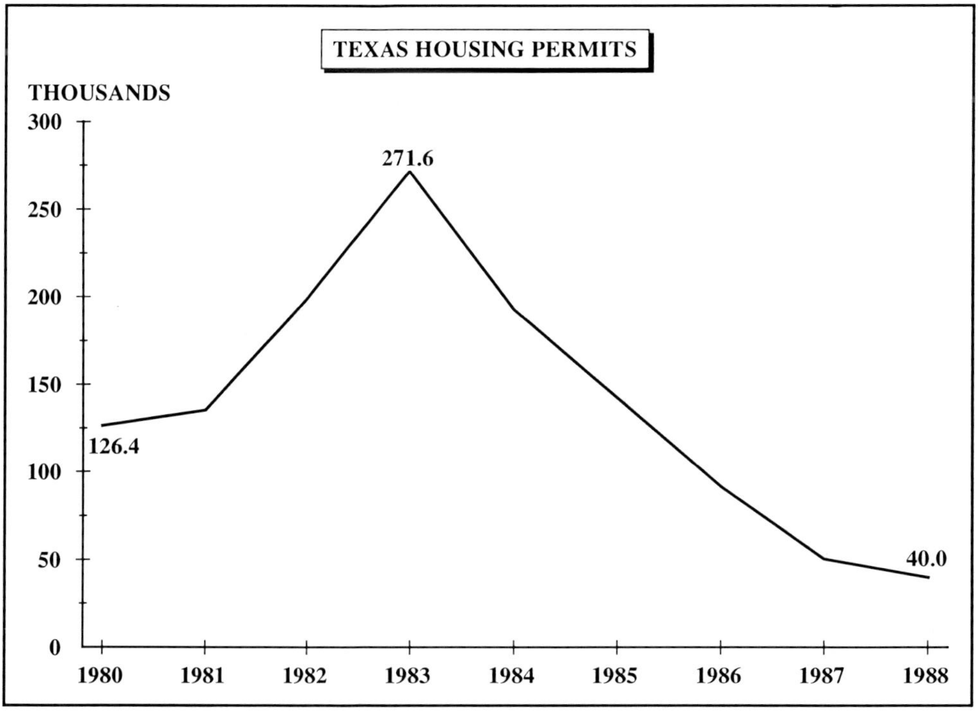

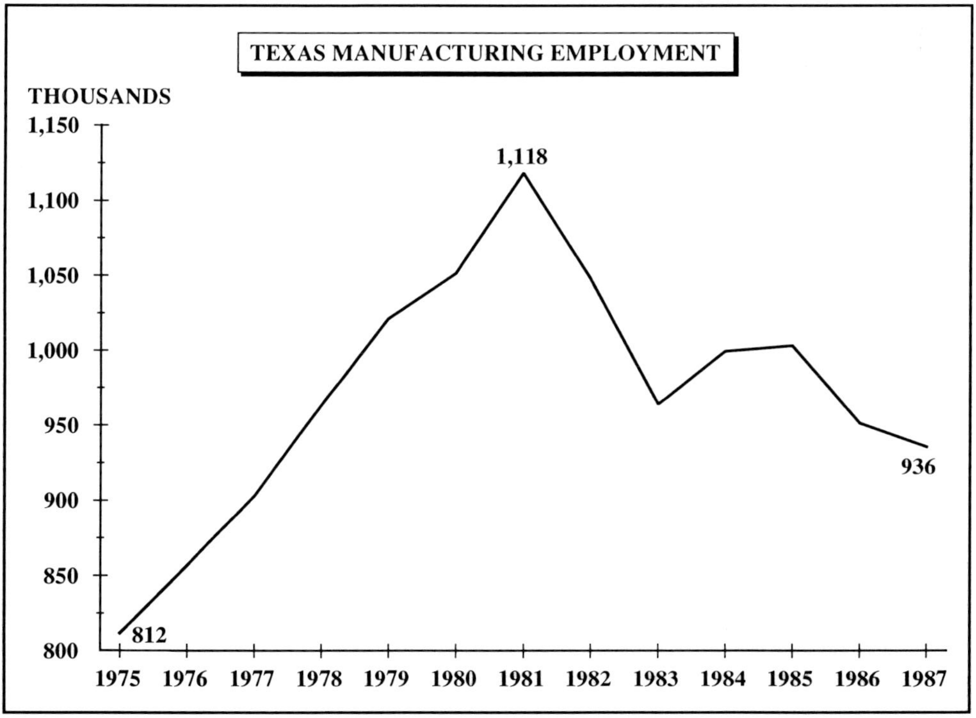

Early scenes from the oil patch.

Photos courtesy: The Texas Collection, Baylor University

HOUSTON SKYLINE—

Photo courtesy: Robert M. Eury/Central Houston, Inc.

Son!! We built some space.

Photo courtesy: Dallas Chamber of Commerce

DALLAS SKYLINE—

New energy for Texas: The South Texas Project

Photo courtesy: Central Power & Light

Photo by: C. Kean, courtesy of Texas State Technical Institute

Education and technology: The future of Texas--a laser refraction experiment at Texas State Technical Institute.

Photo courtesy: The Perot Group

As the 1980s end, the first plane lands at Fort Worth Alliance Airport.

would enjoy one of their more stable periods during 1983 and 1984. That was the amazing thing; oil prices just sat there, swinging from maybe $29 to $27 and back again for what seemed like forever.

Basically, the recovery came because oil didn't do anything and some other things grew. Remember that we were putting up about 200,000 housing units a year, not to mention office towers, retail centers, warehouses, mini-storage buildings, fast food facilities, and just about anything else you can imagine. We probably had a few barn raisings thrown in, and I wouldn't be surprised if we even brought a few more outhouses on line as well. In the summer of 1983, the *Dallas Morning News* ran a story entitled "Lenders Rush Back to Real Estate." The six little words in that headline told us just about all that needed to be said about that period. Of course, I'm going to say quite a bit more. Back when I was still in math school, I figured out that if some things are flat and others are going up, then the average is going up! This less than brilliant conclusion really explains our recovery in 1983-1985. Oil was flat, and real estate and a few other things were expanding. Add 'em all up, and you get a decent, if not sustainable, business upswing.

With the advantage of hindsight, this three-year period may best be described as one of transition, readjustment, and all-out real estate frenzy. A number of noteworthy economic events occurred during this time that would set the stage for many elements of the future of Texas. In retrospect, however, most of them represented bridges from the old to the new. My own universe was also in a state of transition. Although I wasn't getting any taller (unfortunately), my profile was rising considerably. I was rapidly getting in the middle of it all, and loving every minute.

In April of 1983, the board of Dallas Area Rapid Transit (DART) approved public transit rail plans. A year later, funds to begin development of the Dallas rail system would be approved. Nonetheless, this initiative became mired in enormous political and beaurocratic difficulties a few years later. I would end up working on efforts to revive it during the latter part of the 1980s. I would also find myself involved in a much more ambitious plan to initiate high speed rail service among the major cities within the state. One thing I learned along the way was that competitiveness for new jobs requires us to plan for new infrastructure (water, utilities, transportation, etc.) years before we need it.

The divestiture of AT&T, and the consequent cutting loose of an independent Southwestern Bell, moved along in 1983 and became a real deal in 1984.

Some very large bank mergers took place in this period as well. The first of the local giants to join forces were Dallas-based Inter-First (formerly First International Bancshares) and Fort Worth's First United Bancorporation. At the time of its approval in April of 1983, this one shattered previous records and was the largest merger of banking organizations in Texas history. Less than a year later, a significant linkage would be forged between Houston's Bank of the Southwest and Mercantile Bank in Dallas. Both of these institutions had been around a long time and were among the leaders in their respective cities. This marriage gave us MBank, MCorp, and a lot of talk about "Momentum." As the 1980s progressed, this financial organization went from Big Mo to Little Mo to No Mo. After a very rocky ride, most of it would be swallowed up by Bank One, a large banking group based in Columbus, Ohio. As a reminder of Old Mo, however, a few survivors are still scattered around the state. They are affectionately known as the "MBank orphans."

Although we didn't know it at the time, we got an even more telling glimpse into the future of our financial world in October, 1983. The scene was the oil-rich-turned-oil-poor Permian Basin. Midland, while still one of the richest places on the planet, was really feeling the pain from the oil glut. The banks were up to their eyeballs in energy loans, and the drillers were not even up to their ankles in money to meet the payments. In an effort to shore up the ailing First National Bank of Midland, the Federal Deposit Insurance Corporation (FDIC) pumped in a $100 million loan on October 13. Only a few days later, the abortive rescue operation failed, and the once proud and profitable First Midland was acquired by Republic. This oil-related collapse, along with that of Penn Square in Oklahoma, received a great deal of publicity back then. There was hardly a doubt in anyone's mind that it would be the biggest financial bailout to ever occur in the empire known as Texas. While a few other banks in the state went down as well, a casualty of that magnitude was clearly thought of as a one-shot deal brought on by a unique set of circumstances that would never again be repeated. No one foresaw that, less than five years later, the acquiring bank would itself fall by the wayside, be the subject of a multi-billion dollar FDIC bailout, and be taken over by

NCNB, an out-of-state holding company. (As you no doubt know, the "NC" in NCNB stands for North Carolina. You just can't write about Texas these days without getting a lot of other states, and even other countries, involved. Things have really changed.)

This first year of recovery also saw other events that would shape our destiny in fundamental ways. Not ones to be left in the dust, or out of the limelight, two prominent Texans, our flamboyant and popular former Governor John B. Connally and former Lieutenant Governor Ben Barnes, used the tax and financial climate as an opportunity to form a new alliance to engage in real estate development. Boone Pickens, from his base at Mesa Petroleum in Amarillo, made his unsuccessful, but extremely profitable, run at Gulf Oil, the most highly publicized of his many acquisition attempts, in the fall of 1983. It was also about then that a referendum to build toll roads in Houston was approved. Toward the end of the 1980s, I would be actively involved in refunding efforts needed to complete the later phases of this ambitious project. By that point, of course, population and employment figures had fallen far below the rosy expectations that existed when the debt was initially issued. We were successful in that endeavor, however, and the ground breaking on the new sections has already taken place. Lest we forget, 1983 was also the year that MCC announced that it was bringing some serious thinkers and tinkerers to Austin.

When it rains, it pours. An entire book, or perhaps an entire set of encyclopedias, could be written about the natural disasters that occurred in the state in the 1980s. Droughts, floods, storms, freezes, and tornadoes all had their day. They also had their economic impacts, inserting random devastation into an already chaotic business environment. Hurricane Alicia blew through the Texas Gulf Coast with destructive abandon in mid-August, severely damaging Galveston's Seawall Boulevard. Before all was said and done, downtown Houston came to resemble a ghost town in its wake, with streets covered in blankets of glass. During that same month, Southwest Airlines flew in on a much brighter note, announcing the largest quarterly profit in its entire history and bucking the general industry earnings patterns at the time. We also learned during that month that many of the larger banks were doing fairly well and that the rate of Texas bank failures had dropped.

By October, the unemployment rate dipped to 6.9%, its lowest level since May of 1982, confirming for many that Texas had joined the rest of the nation in fashioning an economic recovery. Within four months, we would see the rate fall below 6.0%. Although it is largely forgotten now, this comeback was sufficient to have most incumbent politicians "running on their records" in the 1984 elections. By then, there were about 7 million folks with all kinds of jobs in Texas, and some of these guys wanted credit for all of them.

My world was rapidly expanding during 1983. I wrote a lot of columns and articles, gave more speeches than I would have thought possible a year earlier, built more and bigger models, and became entrenched in the "real world" use of our information by corporate and governmental groups. My initial prognostications about the oil industry were correct, and folks were beginning to pay almost too much attention to what I had to say.

Some of my earliest experiences as a forecasting consultant came with some of the electric utilities of Texas. They remain among our largest clients to this day. We work with them on rate cases, projections of energy usage and customers, economic development initiatives, and a variety of other projects. One of my initial encounters with many of the good folks who help supply the power to run the state was in July of 1983, when I gave a seminar on the Texas economy during a major public utility conference in Dallas. As best I recall, I was fearlessly (well, almost) optimistic about our short-term prospects. After the precipitous declines during 1982, I was calling for renewed growth over the next two years, though not at the tremendous rates enjoyed during the oil boom. This forecast, of course, was tempered with the caveat that the picture could change quickly and dramatically should the price of oil tumble.

A bunch of people throughout the state were glad to see me come down on the positive side of things. I guess there was some concern within the ranks that, based on my first forecast, I would just be another one of those perpetual naysaying bears who always go around spouting "gloom and doom." Far from it. Anybody who knows me will readily testify that I'm a perpetual optimist at heart. In fact, it had taken an overwhelming body of evidence for me to call that downturn in 1982. If my first forecast gave me credibility and a reputation for some halfway decent insights, my later ones led folks to know that, good or bad, I would call 'em like I saw 'em.

At the time I spoke at that utility conference, I was also assisting Brazos Electric Cooperative, a power-generating consortium of rural electric cooperatives and cities, in their forecasting and survey efforts. I was still a neophyte in this field and just beginning to learn the ropes. The project constituted my first opportunity to personally use my economic models in such an applied setting, something I would do thousands and thousands of times throughout the country over the course of the 1980s. It was also one of the first times it dawned on me that the models that we developed could be used for major investment decisions, loan programs, federal policies, and resource planning. That's a little scary. Brazos remains a very good client, and we work with them regularly in updating and refining their forecasts.

As I was getting my feet wet in this effort, both the federal and state governments were starting to require economic models to support utility forecasts. (Given my occupation, that didn't exactly break my heart!) In days gone by, the engineering firms that did the system planning and design work (transmission lines, cables, sub-stations, and all of that complicated stuff) typically also did the forecasting of future power requirements. They used trend lines of historic growth. Trend lines are basically simple statistical models that take historical patterns and extend them out over time. They work real well as long as the future is pretty much the same as the past. If the 1970s and 1980s have taught us anything, however, they have certainly taught us that trend lines don't work. The mere passage of time doesn't explain much of anything. The economy is just too volatile to trust it all to history. Understanding the past is vitally important, but it's only part of the process. We have to look at all of the surrounding factors, which is what economic models do best, in trying to come up with prognostications about the future.

My first endeavor as a utility forecaster also gave me my first taste of a real turf battle. (We have them all the time in academia, but those don't count.) As you can imagine, the engineers did not view the invasion of the economists with tremendous joy. We held face-to-face meetings, however, and they quickly came to realize that I respected their professional judgment, backed by years of experience in the field, and that I was more than willing to work with them to combine the best of my information and theirs into a good forecast. We still laugh about some of those early, rather heated, discussions whenever we get together.

It was also at this point in time that I got my initial taste of Washington bureaucracy. The forecast had to be approved by the

Rural Electric Administration, a division of the U.S. Department of Agriculture. The process involved a lot of red tape, meetings, and seemingly endless discussions over what I, as an impatient youngster, considered to be largely inconsequential matters. I got to see firsthand how cumbersome the federal bureaucracy can be. The new guidelines regarding the use of models in the forecasting process were in their preliminary stages of development at that point in time. When we got together to go over another batch of projections in 1989 (six years later!), the final approvals had still not come through.

I did not react well at all to my early experiences in this realm. I like to do a project, do it right, finish it, get results, and move on to the next one. I'm very much a doer, and very much not a paper shuffler. Over time, though, I did become a little more patient and understanding of bureautic processes and legal systems and, armed with that patience, a little more adept at getting things done. There is a fine line that must be walked to be successful in this arena. You have to be tolerant enough to allow the system to work (believe it or not, it usually does), but not so patient that you get swallowed up in the process itself and lose sight of the overall objective. When I believe in something, I'm extremely aggressive. I still have a reputation for turning things completely upside down when necessary. I hope I never lose that one.

As we moved boldly into 1984, the second year of our tenuous recovery, it was obvious that we were coming back. It was especially apparent, however, that our fundamental economic structure was changing dramatically. I was the self-appointed disciple of diversification, preaching my gospel to anyone who would listen or, at least, pretend to. In January of that year, I wrote an economic outlook article (my second) for *Texas Business* magazine. Unfortunately, that truly outstanding publication is no longer with us; it was one of the innumerable casualties of the downturns in the very business that it covered so well. At any rate, I offered a fairly optimistic short-term forecast, recounting the gains we had already made in many sectors during 1983, and forecasting further growth in 1984. Despite this relatively upbeat synopsis, the article was entitled "No Longer Wild and Free," a phrase which pretty much sums up the essence of the Texas economy during the transitional period of the 1980s. My main point was that we would not again, in all likelihood, see the galloping gait that we maintained during the 1970s, but that we were moving along again at a very nice trot.

With a decreasing dependence on oil and an increasingly diversified economy, we could expect to win quite a few races (even if we didn't shatter too many track records along the way).

I likened us to a great, wild stallion, akin to the graceful and powerful one that adorns the back cover of this book. (In case you weren't sure, I'm the short guy in front!) Running wild, he is a beautiful thing to behold. But as any horseflesh-loving Texan knows, effective training of such a magnificent beast is essential to harness his full potential. The aim is not to break his spirit, for that would entirely defeat the purpose of training. Rather, the objective is to productively channel his boundless energy and indomitable spirit.

By early 1984, I saw a striking similarity between the life of a great stallion and the path that was confronting the Texas economy. Our generations of unbridled expansion gave rise to the tremendous spirit that, among other things, spawned the legendary Texas tycoons. But now we had to be smarter and more focused and not just rely on undomesticated energy, literally and figuratively. It was becoming clear that Texans, like the stallion, would have to train and redirect ourselves in order to achieve our potential destiny. It is an image that I enjoyed creating at the time, and one that still holds today.

Whatever else would happen, 1984 certainly began with a bang. In the week prior to New Year's, the news leaked out that Pennzoil was about to acquire Getty Oil, the surviving legacy of J. Paul Getty. Mr. Getty, purportedly America's first billionaire, was a pioneer of the concept of drilling for oil on Wall Street. In the Depression era market, proven reserves could be obtained a lot more cost-effectively by buying shares of companies with "oil in the ground" than going after them via the more expensive and risky method that involves roughnecks, drill bits, and perspiration.

The Pennzoil quest was admittedly a little bit like David going after Goliath, but David did win that conflict. Pennzoil, a Texas firm based in Houston and headed by Hugh Liedtke, had an interesting and colorful history that spanned several states and several generations. Mr. Liedtke himself is one of those great characters that only Texas can generate, a tough oil baron who had once been a young wildcatter in Midland with another young Texan by the name of George Bush. With this bold acquisition of Getty, Pennzoil was looking to become a major player in the oil industry. We have all been familiar with those famous little yellow cans for years, but have not seen similar big yellow signs alongside those of Exxon, Texaco, Shell, Chevron, and others at the major exits lining the interstate highways of the land. With the Getty assets in tow, including a fleet of stations and a veritable ocean of oil in the ground, Mr. Liedtke and his firm would join the elite group of truly major oil companies. In an era of mergers and acquisitions that far exceeded anything that J. Paul Getty could imagine, the folks at Pennzoil hoped to perform the ultimate coup in drilling for oil on Wall Street.

A few days into 1984, the official merger plans were announced with considerable fanfare. A couple of days later, the business world was stunned by the news that Texaco had managed to step in and mess up the deal, and was in the process of acquiring Getty for itself. Texaco had its eye on Getty's precious reserves. For all its enormous success in marketing petroleum over the years, Texaco had never matched its rivals in exploration. This deal would go a long way toward evening the score. This merger represented the largest takeover in U.S. history and set in motion a colossal legal battle that would totally redefine the environment in which corporate America functions. More than four years later, I would find myself still working on research endeavors related to the conclusion of this drama. Before all the dust settled, the largest judgment in history and the largest settlement ever paid would come down through the courts in this ultimate Texas-style litigation. The case would bring in its wake one of the most massive bankruptcies of all time, and a check so big that the Federal Reserve had to process it in four parts. It would also bring a ferocious clamor for fundamental judicial reform within the state.

One other event with substantial implications for the state also occurred in this initial month of 1984. This time, the culprit was not oil company executives sitting in posh confines in New York, California, and Texas, nor was it their lawyers and investment bankers that collect fortunes in fees from the merger and acquisition game. It was a character that has had a very long run, playing a variety of roles, on the Texas stage. I'm talking about good old Mother Nature. Her current appearance was in the guise of a major freeze that gripped large portions of Texas and inflicted severe damage on the crops in the lower Rio Grande Valley. I remember this event for several reasons. I had just recently visited the Valley, in October of 1983, to present the first forecast from our new model of this region.

My memory of that October trip to the Valley is vivid because of its inspirational effect on me as we all moved forward through the treacherous waters of Texas in the 1980s. At the time, the peso had collapsed and retail trade in the area had suffered dramatically. The oil industry was mired in difficulty, which adversely impacted both South Texas and Mexico. There were also export problems associated with certain pesticides and other impediments to the agricultural economy of the region. Unemployment rates in the Valley were at historic highs, and there were many other signs of economic difficulty.

Despite its problems, the Valley clearly had enormous potential and promise. Its population base, wage structure, fertile soil, climate, and many other factors combined to make it an area ripe with economic opportunity. A few years earlier, when oil prices were rocketing into the stratosphere, it had been known as Magic Valley. Before the fall, it had become an investor's Mecca. In addition to presenting my forecast, I was asked to say a few words at the groundbreaking of a major new office facility in McAllen, anchored by a banking concern. (Back then, people still opened new banks.) The mover and shaker behind this gutsy development effort, who had the determination to see it through in the face of such a major regional downturn, was a young man by the name of Jay Palmer. To see an entrepreneurial endeavor of this nature begin in the midst of the malaise in the Valley was concrete testimony to the spirit that carried most of Texas throughout our economic difficulties.

I will be the first to admit that I was skeptical about the prospects for this ambitious undertaking, and I kept close tabs on its progress. To say the least, it was a squeaker. A few years later, I would speak at the ribbon cutting of the new facility and would return to the Valley many subsequent times to assist in various business development endeavors. I would also visit the region on several occasions to work with and promote the burgeoning maquiladora program. Maquiladoras are plants in Mexico that make use of low wage labor for assembly operations and other tasks requiring relatively unskilled workers. Through special tariff relationships, distribution takes place through the United States. Most of the facilities are presently concentrated along the border, in places like Matamoros, Reynosa, Nuevo Laredo, and Juarez. Their growth has been genuinely explosive, and a lot of dollars and jobs find their way over to this side of the border.

As I stood up to speak and present my forecast on that night in October of 1983, I felt an awesome responsibility to provide at least some measure of hope and encouragement in the face of the lingering problems confronting this tropical paradise. Maquilas were in their infancy then, and the folks in McAllen, Brownsville, Harlingen, and the rest of that unique and populous territory had really taken it on the chin. I talked of the assets of the Valley, of its long-term potential, and of the likelihood of a reasonable recovery in 1984 if the crops just didn't freeze. . . . Less than three months later, the crops froze.

The problems associated with a freeze in the Valley are compounded by the fact that one of the principal local cash crops is citrus. Unlike potatoes or money, lemons, limes, grapefruit, and oranges grow on trees. Once destroyed, it takes a new batch of them three to six years to bear fruit. The region would suffer two more blitzes from Texas winters in the 1980s, including a really devastating one as the decade drew to a close. Nevertheless, when the real Texas economic recovery began in earnest in late 1987, the Valley would be one of the places that led the way in the creation of new jobs. (Jay and Martha Palmer and I would also become good friends along the way. One of my first tasks of the 1990s was to venture down to McAllen to speak at the groundbreaking of a large manufacturing facility in a brand new industrial park. The developer was, you guessed it, Jay Palmer.)

The Pennzoil-Texaco battle was again claiming the economic headlines. By this point, Hugh Liedtke had filed a multibillion-dollar lawsuit in a Delaware court. Pennzoil had at least temporarily lost the dream of making it to the major leagues, and the company was itching for another turn at bat. In one of the grandest curve balls ever thrown, the company used a legal loophole to move the litigation to Houston. That move changed the rules of the game more than lights at Wrigley Field and designated hitters combined. I'll keep you posted on this one as we move along. Like a trainload of Tootsie Rolls, it lasts a long, long time.

Real estate development buzzed along in Texas, with Dallas and Houston leading the nation in many categories. When statistics were released in the spring on county population patterns, it turned out that, during the first part of the 1980s, Texas topped the list. The top four fastest growing counties in the entire country were Denton (just north of Dallas), Montgomery (just north of Houston), Ector (Odessa), and Fort Bend (southwest of

Houston). Much to the chagrin of those of us in the forecasting business, this information comes out with a considerable lag. We were reading headlines that still reflected the oil boom. Unfortunately, the release of numbers to the press can significantly affect what people think, even if they are dated and the world has been dramatically altered in the meantime. The stories surrounding this report found their way into more than a few loan files in the financial institutions of the state.

In June, General Motors acquired Electronic Data Services (EDS), the giant and innovative Texas software company founded and built by H. Ross Perot. A few years later, the very public separation of Mr. Perot from this merged entity attracted enormous attention and netted him a few hundred million dollars. In keeping with the astuteness that has characterized his entire career and the heritage of Texas legends, he turned around, seized the moment, and invested heavily in a Texas economy fraught with opportunity.

As 1984 progressed, there was an excess of oil in the world market largely as a result of the Persian Gulf War between Iran and Iraq. The OPEC countries tried to deal with this phenomenon, but there was dissension among their faltering ranks with regard to price and production quotas. By the beginning of 1985, prices were slipping to some extent, but generally remained in that stubbornly persistent $27-$29 per barrel range. Most prognosticators were expecting 1985 to be a good year for Texas banks, and the attitude within the state was generally pretty good.

Although I couldn't begin to appreciate its significance at the time, the high point of my year, from the vantage point of hindsight, had to be "The Speech." I address tens of thousands of people in a typical month and easily made more than 1,000 appearances of various kinds in the 1980s. To this day, however, a hundred or more people a year will write letters or come up to chat about "The Speech." There's never any doubt which one they're talking about: The Texas Lyceum; Loews Anatole; Dallas, Texas; September, 1984.

The Lyceum has become something of a Texas institution. It was largely the brainchild of one Tieman H. "Skipper" Dippel, banker from Brenham (also the home of Blue Bell Ice Cream) and Texas patriot extraordinaire. Whenever it's time to fight the good fight for the betterment of the state, you can depend on Skipper to step in the ring. In fact, you couldn't keep him out if you tried. (He is also one of the people who most encouraged me to write this book.)

These days, the Lyceum doesn't have the money that it did during those first few terrific years. It still serves a very useful purpose, though, and I participate as often as I possibly can. Nowadays, we mostly talk to ourselves. Like so many other things in Texas, the organization can no longer pull off tremendous entravaganzas. The collapse of oil and real estate really kicked the wealth base of the state in the teeth. During those initial convocations, however, the Lyceum brought in some serious heavyweights.

In 1984, the topic was "High Tech." Those words had an almost mystic quality in Texas at the time. A few of us who had been hammering away at the diversification theme were beginning to penetrate the collective psyche, if not of the man on the street or the drilling platform, at least of the state's intelligentsia. Oil was having problems, but we had MCC, NASA, Texas Instruments, Tracor, a bunch of sophisticated aerospace companies, several classy medical complexes, Henry Cisneros' oratory, and at least a truckload of folks who could say "I-35 Corridor" with a straight face.

Every place I visited at the time, from major urban centers to small rural communities, I was asked how they should go about getting some of that "high tech" stuff. In many cases, these lush garden spots of America were 200 miles from anywhere and had none of the amenities and infrastructure required by firms in electronics, biotechnology, or avionics. That little detail didn't matter at all, though. Once we had convinced local leaders of the benefits of diversification, they wanted a simple, neat, and quick solution. People wanted one strategy to cover everything and everybody. They wanted to cure their ills, and "high tech" was the miracle elixir that all the medicine men were peddling. Folks still had a lot to learn, but at least they had signed up for the class.

The participants in the 1984 Texas Lyceum included ABC commentator Ted Koppel, former British Prime Minister Edward Heath, and Daniel Bell, a prominent Harvard professor. Like I said, they hauled in some serious talent. By the time it got around to me, they had heard from a lot of panels who had reached a general concensus of "Yep! You've found the answer."

My roll was that of Friday night speaker at a Special Session (not to be confused with those in the legislature). I was to present the results of my newly created model of high tech potential in Texas. At the time, the system was the only one of its kind in the world. People were real excited. The Short Kid (that's me) was about to stand up and tell them that the numbers worked; all they had to do was go for it. But my message didn't quite turn out the way it was supposed to. I didn't follow the script.

I'm not sure how large the crowd was that night. Judging from the amount of food at the back of the room, the number of chairs, and the time I spent jawing around afterwards, I'd say it was around 300-400. Judging from the people from every corner of Texas who have since recounted the evening to me and told me they were there, I'd say about 300,000-400,000. I do know that the crowd included many of the most prominent and influential people in the state. I also recall that the food was pretty good.

My own recollection of the evening is not nearly as vivid as that of others, some of whom weren't even there. It was one of the dozen or so speeches I gave that month. After all, September and October are the times when most companies are planning for the next year, and the old calendar tends to get pretty crowded for a forecaster. I do remember that I had some transparencies to show. I never use visual aids of that sort, but the people doing the program felt it was really important for some reason that I forget. I also recall that I received an absolutely brutal introduction from Gary Wood, my good friend who now heads the Texas Research League. I expected nothing less. Strangely enough, the primary thing that sticks in my mind is the sound system. Standing behind the microphone, I was greeted with a very high pitched sound that made it difficult to think and left me with a headache for several days afterward.

Fortunately, the crowd couldn't hear that terrible noise, but they did hear what I had to say. That may have been worse. After a few jokes, some of which were aimed at Gary, I dutifully went through the various definitions the government had given us for "high tech" and exactly which industries fit the bill. I then talked about what their potential was, and wasn't, for Texas. It was the "wasn't" that got folks' attention.

The definition that best fits what everybody thinks of when high tech is mentioned is one that designates an industry as technologically oriented if it spends at least twice as much (in percentage terms) as the national average on research and development. According to this standard, there are only six categories that qualify: microelectronics, aircraft, computers, drugs (including biotechnology), telecommunications, and space. That pretty well sums up the old "high tech" ball game. At the time, these sectors constituted roughly 2.5% of business activity in Texas. They had excellent growth potential, however, and I forecasted that, by the turn of the century, they might be all the way up to 3.5% or even 4.0%. On the surface, that was a very bullish prediction. To gain that much "market share," they would have to expand a whole lot faster than anything else.

My basic theme was that high tech was certainly part of the answer, but not all of it. The problem was simply that these industries were not big enough to replace what we were losing in drilling, oil field equipment, steel mills, and the other vestiges of our vast energy complex. Technology firms are great and we should vigorously pursue them. They normally don't pollute the environment too much; they bring in high-paying jobs and well-educated citizens; they enhance community profiles; they are good for our egos. But if Texas was to meet the challenge of the future, we had to go after not only high tech, but also food processing, tourism, business services, basic industrial machinery, paper, and a bunch of other stuff that wasn't nearly as sexy as silicon chips, semiconductors, and fiber optics. Moreover, not every place in Texas could expect to be an exploding center of "high tech" activity. In fact, there were precious few that would meet the specs.

In short, I burst the bubble. I sent everyone back to work. I said that it wouldn't be easy, and that the same thing wouldn't work everywhere. It was a sobering message, but I think it helped get us on the right track. That made two times that I had been the bearer of bad news. The first time, nobody listened. The second time, they did.

There have probably been nights when I have been funnier. There have hopefully been nights when I have been more insightful. There have been few, if any, nights, however, when I have struck a chord more resonantly than that Friday evening in September, 1984. For me, the highlight of 1984 came on February 4, when my second daughter, Bethany Rae, was born. For a lot of folks, however, what they remember is "The Speech."

Viewed in retrospect, 1985 can be seen as a year of transition. The recovery within Texas continued throughout most of the year, but there were increasing rumblings about more oil problems, office vacancies, lower apartment occupancy, and similar early indications of changes in the real estate development situation. Rumors were hot and heavy about the problems of Global Marine, a large company engaged in offshore drilling. In May of 1985, the company found itself denying rumors of an imminent filing for protection under Chapter 11 of the Federal Bankruptcy Code. This firm had been off to a fast start in the early 1980s, when offshore drilling was the hottest thing going. It had engaged in an aggressive investment program that was the envy of the industry. Banks were clamoring and lobbying to be a part of the financing package. All that it took to make this deal work was (1) the leasing of approximately 100% of the rigs in the Gulf of Mexico and (2) an oil price of $90 or so per barrel by 1990. At the time of the handshakes and paper signings, this plan was viewed as highly prudent and conservative. After all, the lease rate for offshore rigs had been 100% practically since the Ice Age. Given an environment in which "$85 in '85" was viewed as a distinct possibility, "$90 in '90" seemed like a lead pipe cinch. By mid-1985, however, the climate had changed considerably, leaving Global Marine a bit high and dry.

On the Middle East front, the OPEC countries continued their discord, with Sheik Yamani being particularly critical of the "off the books" discounting that was taking place among some member nations. Mexico reduced its oil prices in July, but on the whole prices held up reasonably well.

During that same scorching and humid summer month, in a small, packed Houston courtroom, the Pennzoil-Texaco trial began. It was a battle of flamboyant attorneys. Pennzoil's lead attorney was the legendary Joe Jamail, the very model of a modern Texas trial lawyer. Before all was said and done, he managed to put the state of New York, Wall Street, and a multitude of fast talking Yankee lawyers and bankers on trial in front of a group of perspiring Houstonians who were no longer the talk of the economic world. Texaco's chief counsel, Richard B. "Dick" Miller, had a reputation for "betting the company." He never had a bigger opportunity.

In September, things at OPEC took a turn that would affect the next few years significantly. For quite some time, the limited unity that OPEC was able to sustain had come largely because of Saudi Arabia's role as a "swing" producer. The Saudis would basically evaluate how much the other countries were cheating on their quotas and adjust their production accordingly. In September of 1985, however, they decided to cease playing this role and reclaim what they considered to be their appropriate market share. Once this line was drawn in the sand, the stage was set for dramatic oil price declines. (By the way, a lot of the OPEC countries that monitor compliance get their data on petroleum production from our intelligence sources. They don't trust each other.)

Throughout this period, the fortunes of the Mexican economy were also in jeopardy. The primary asset this nation has for dealing with myriad economic and demographic concerns is its huge oil reserves. With markets weakening, the pressure could only mount. Texas shares a huge border with Mexico and our fortunes are closely tied to the health of this border economy. By November, the peso had reached 440 to the dollar (it would fall much further over the next few years). I used to emphasize in my speeches that the long-term future of Texas hinged on three major challenges and that oil, for all of its publicity, was only third among them. The second most important factor was water. The very first concern was Mexico.

All of these topics were in the news as 1985 was winding down. The peso was falling like a rock, and dangers of another oil glut and another round of price reductions were looming. At about the same time, on the positive side of the ledger, the state water plan was approved. I have had several opportunities to defend this program and work on revisions for the new structure that was recently adopted. Through careful resource planning, we should be able to respond to most of the water needs for new business and industrial development, while protecting our vital ecosystem, for the foreseeable future.

One of the most important dramas to take place during the midst of the 1983-85 recovery phase revolved around efforts to reform the education system in Texas. While "oil, water, and Mexico" may be our long-term concerns, education is a dominant issue for all times, including today. The central figure of this effort was H. Ross Perot, who chaired a committee appointed by Governor Mark White to suggest reforms to improve the system. (The democrats had reclaimed the Governor's Mansion in 1982, with then Attorney General White defeating incumbent Bill Clements.) To say that a good deal of controversy swirled around this initiative is putting it mildly, but ultimately a set of reforms were enacted. The biggest issue was the "No pass-No play" stricture, which dealt a major blow to the proud Texas tradition of taking care of high school football players who often scored higher on the playing fields than in the classroom. It was a direct attack on one of Texas' most sacred cows. It was ultimately passed, although not without a good fight. As of today, overall quality within the system has improved moderately, and efforts to increase the emphasis on academics seem to have paid off. While some of the administrative mechanisms from this program were cumbersome and frustrating, the early results indicate that a significant first step was made.

Texans really are serious about their high school football, and Friday Night Fever reaches epidemic proportions by November of each year. It really doesn't matter who wins or who loses, as long as our side wins. To my surprise, I discovered in my various journeys that our football fanaticism can play a role in economic development initiatives as well. I have long been a proponent of regional cooperation, and have been instrumental in organizing efforts of this nature throughout Texas. Every time I start out in this direction, I inevitably find intense rivalry between neighboring towns. If it goes beyond friendly competition and civic pride, I always try to get to the bottom of it and find out what the real problem is. More often than not, it comes down to a referee's call, a field goal at the last second, a cheap shot on an All-District quarterback, or some other memory of gridiron glory in one town and agony in the other. Those legendary teams fielded by Paul Tyson at Waco High seriously bruised the egos of virtually every town of any size in Central Texas. He didn't just beat them; he humiliated them. Several decades later, those memories still serve as a stumbling block to cooperative endeavors.

Education has remained a major concern throughout the 1980s, although the emphasis has sadly shifted more toward money than anything else. The courts have recently held that the property tax mechanism traditionally used to fund Texas schools is unconstitutional because of its discriminatory treatment of poorer districts. The cost to fix these inequities could well be in the billions of dollars. (Nothing is small in Texas.) This decision brought the need for major changes to a head. As the 1990s began, the legislature would still be grappling with this most difficult issue.

Of even more significance than the immediate financing demands of our vast school system, however, is the desperate need for further academic enhancement and the essential task of providing vocational and technical training to insure competent Texas-grown workers for the new and increasingly complex industrial economy of the future. This concern is universal, and certainly not within the private domain of the Lone Star State. In our case, it may be even more crucial than elsewhere, as we make our belated transition from an economy of the ground to an economy of the mind. In the period when the reform movement began in earnest, we were still "surviving." I'll say a little more about this issue later, when we get down to the "conquering" part.

Economic development and our attempts to diversify represented one bright star on the horizon as the first half of the 1980s wound down. One interesting effort on that front during 1984 and 1985 was the enormous Texas effort to woo General Motors in the site selection for its proposed Saturn plant. The giant firm from Detroit turned out to be a reluctant bridegroom, ultimately building the facility in a small town in Tennessee. Jilted or not, we learned a great deal from the experience.

Texas had done very little in the way of aggressive economic development in the 1970s. Why should we? The oil boom and overall prosperity were sufficient to lure a great deal of activity to the state, with scarcely anyone having to lift a finger. The concept of funding programs of this nature was almost as foreign to us as goods produced in Japan, West Germany, or even Massachusetts. We ranked at or near the bottom of the nation in virtually every category of spending for new development. Nonetheless, we ranked at or near the top in new companies, relocations, expansions, job growth, and just about any other barometer you cared to read.

As the recession began, however, it was obvious that creating jobs for the future and attracting new industry into the state was going to require a lot of hard work. We could no longer rely solely on natural resources, Lyndon Johnson, and Sam Rayburn. We were entering a new era in which human resources would dominate, and LBJ and Mr. Sam were no longer with us. Communities throughout the state began to go out of their way to seek new industry, and we learned the rules of the game with regard to incentives and other factors that played a major role in economic development. We even went so far as to mimic successful approaches from other states and have folks from the East Coast come down here to tell us how it was done. Desperate times called for desperate measures.

While the Saturn romance eventually fizzled, many regions within the state cut their teeth on this effort and became much more knowledgeable of the nature of such initiatives. It had indeed been a grand cause for a while. It seemed like every office I went into in Austin had an obligatory manila folder on the desk with "Saturn" written across it. (I always suspected that some of them were empty.) Even though our courtship turned out to be a nonevent, it was far from an exercise in futility.

Through my work as the assembler and analyzer of data, I became a sort of gatekeeper to the cathedral of information about every corner of the state. We also had access to information from other parts of the country, and, thus, began to be involved quite actively with various communities in seeking new business opportunities. Our work on economic development, strategic planning, site selection, and related issues is something that we view with a considerable sense of satisfaction. To see hard-hit cities, such as Beaumont, Longview, Midland, and Houston, respond to the challenge in creative and innovative ways has been enormously gratifying. Although the sledding is tough at times, it has been very satisfying to assist local leaders in learning how to be involved in economic development and to work with regional agencies, utilities, and business leaders throughout the state in concerted efforts to make things happen.

There is a certain irony to the fact that we launched the largest such project ever undertaken at the offices of the East Texas Council of Governments (ETCOG) in Kilgore. Going back to that area, it was very difficult for me to imagine that Kilgore, the site of the greatest oil bonanza the state has ever seen and the symbol of prosperity unbounded throughout my youth, could now be a small, depressed community much in need of a shot in the arm. The chance to be in this place at this time with this opportunity makes the countless hours of work, task force meetings, and riding in all types of vehicles worthwhile and, in fact, sheer pleasure. (It also gave me a few chances to get some ribs at the Country Tavern.)

Let's venture back to the end of 1985, as the calm before the storm was rapidly dissipating. In mid-November, the jury in that infamous Houston courtroom shocked the world by finding for the plaintiff and rendering a judgment of more than $10.5 billion in favor of Pennzoil. This amount was enough to allow the entire Getty reserve to be rediscovered and brought into production, with an extra $3 billion thrown in to teach folks from New York a lesson about the importance of handshakes and signatures, especially the former. It was several times higher than the previous record for a litigation judgment, raising the playing field to a whole new level. This verdict would lead to a lot of drama over the next few years, including a bankruptcy filing by Texaco to forestall enforcement of the judgment. For awhile there, it looked like a lot of black and red signs with stars on them might swiftly turn yellow.

The global attention accorded this case brought notoriety to the civil justice system of Texas in ways that would serve as a catalyst to a significant reform movement. While I worked aggressively (and still do) to bring about changes in some of our statutes, I really didn't regard this particular case as being all that relevant to the broader issues of fairness in our litigation process. To my admittedly nonlegal mind, Pennzoil-Texaco seemed to be more a dispute about the sanctity of contracts than one about workers' compensation, product liability, deceptive trade practices, and the other "tort" issues which have clouded the Texas business climate at various points. At any rate, there is little doubt that twelve Houstonians permanently redefined the very fabric of American corporate culture and dealt a stunning blow to Wall Street's merger moguls.

Ironically, as the year drew to a close, there was modest firming in oil prices. Major producers began to post prices in the $28 to $29 per barrel range. Nonetheless, there was a price war brewing between OPEC and certain non-OPEC producers, and anything but harmony within the ranks of the cartel. Texas was about to go into a very difficult year. Oil prices would drop precipitously. There would be horrendous additional job losses. The realization of significant real estate difficulties would begin to surface. We might forget 1983, '84 and '85, but we would certainly remember 1986. It was not going to be a pretty picture.

EIGHT

A Texas-Sized Recession

1986 AND 1987

1986. Nineteen hundred and eighty six. One-nine-eight-six. MCMLXXXVI. No matter how you say it, write it, or even think it, it comes out the same. For many people in many places, it was a fairly ordinary time. The U.S. economy saw real gross national product grow by 2.8%, which is pretty close to the long-term trend. Employment increased by a healthy 2.1%, as the country added about 2 million workers to the ranks. The jobless rate continued to fall in the United States, breaking the 7.0% barrier. In short, the domestic economy had a pretty decent year. To the average guy living in Connecticut, Oregon, or North Dakota, 1986 was probably nothing to write home about.

In Texas, however, the economic devastation was unbelievable. In sharp contrast to the 1970s, the Lone Star State was entering a downturn that was riveting in its pace, its depth, and its breadth. One of Willie Nelson's songs begins with the phrase, "It ain't supposed to be that way." Truer words were never spoken. The year 1986 was the Sesquicentennial of the Republic of Texas. It was supposed to be one big party. It wasn't; not by any stretch of the imagination. It is difficult to talk about, and almost impossible to describe. We will walk through it together, blow by blow. Through that process, I hope that you can gain at least some sense of the events, emotions, and excesses of what was arguably the most difficult of the 150 years that Texas had endured since the Battle of San Jacinto in 1836.

The year began on a horrific note, when the Challenger, one of America's space shuttles, exploded in an enormous ball of fire shortly after lifting off. Space travel had become somewhat routine over the years, to the point that we usually didn't even bother to notice more than casually the latest mission. This particular adventure had drawn a lot of attention, however, because one of the passengers was a high school teacher from Concord, New Hampshire by the name of Christa McAuliffe. During the course of her preparation for the voyage, she had won the hearts of people throughout the world.

Every generation tends to have an event that becomes a point of reference for everything else. For my parents, it was December of 1941. Everyone from that generation can tell you where they were and what they were doing when they received the news about the attack on Pearl Harbor. They recall surrounding factors, conversations with friends, idle comments they overheard, and a sea of minutia about those fateful days. For my generation, the scene shifts ahead approximately twenty-two years and leaves the waters of Oahu for the streets of Dallas. We all vividly recall myriad details surrounding the assassination of President John F. Kennedy in November, 1963. Moving forward another twenty-two years or so, we find ourselves in January, 1986. The stage is the sky over Florida, and the defining moment for another era of American history suddenly and tragically surfaces.

The eyes of the entire country, and, indeed, the world were channeled on the explosion of the space shuttle Challenger. Because of the charismatic appeal of a delightful young educator venturing into parts unknown, the launch was witnessed directly by millions in elementary school classrooms and on television screens around the globe. The death of the crew of seven was an immense human tragedy in the inexorable march of technical progress. It was very much a world-sobering event.

Although no one was even remotely thinking about it at the time, the Challenger disaster would, like so many other disparate factors, come into play in the economic saga of Texas in 1986. To be perfectly blunt, the timing was obviously less than ideal for the

Texas-based National Aeronautics and Space Agency (NASA). Its priority as a federal budget item dropped like a stone, and the subsequent reductions in federal monies would bring additional problems for Houston. At the time of the explosion, however, people's concern was focused not on the economic consequences of this tragedy, nor on the setback in the U.S. space programs which ensued. Rather, as a natural human reaction, there was a heartfelt outpouring of sympathy for the families, and international mourning for the heroes of that ill-fated trek. Such is as it should be.

Although it would not (and should not) receive the concentrated attention accorded the Challenger, an economic disaster of epic proportions was taking shape in Texas. On the oil front, there were new waves of uncertainty and instability rolling in almost every day in early 1986 from the international petroleum markets. As the year began, it was obvious that an OPEC pricing war was virtually inevitable. It also seemed likely that other oil-producing nations would enter the fray as well. Although contract prices for West Texas Intermediate Crude remained over $26 a barrel for most of January, the spot market price had fallen to only slightly above $21 by January 20. A week later, Global Marine's efforts to avoid bankruptcy would prove futile, and the filing for the Chapter 11 bankruptcy reorganization that had been rumored for almost a year would finally take place. It was a sad ending to what was supposed to be a Cinderella story. (This book only has ten chapters. I thought that I would at least spare us one more Chapter 11.)

Meanwhile, in the vast hinterlands of Waco, I had been warning of a potential oil price collapse for months. Since the Saudis had ceased taking up the slack for everybody else in the fall of the previous year, it seemed inevitable. We had been providing our subscribers with scary scenarios to deal with since April of 1985. By this point, I was in constant contact with a global network of company executives, oil traders, market analysts, government officials, and others who were supposed to be in the know. I had been around long enough and been right often enough to earn my spurs. I had also figured out how to read those "shiny rigs." I now had access to an enormous network of people and information that I couldn't have even imagined when I gave my first fearless forecast in 1982. I will freely admit, however, that, while I saw the risks in the oil market well in advance and began warning folks that there was probably a rough ride out there, neither I nor anyone else had a clue of just how bad it was going to be.

Drilling activity began to plummet in January and continued to slide over an extended period of time. By the end of the month, virtually all of the major oil companies had reduced the contract price of Texas oil to $25 a barrel. This number was of particular significance, as it represented the bottom price that had been assumed in calculating the revenue stream on which to base the state budget. When the market slid even lower, things went south on a fast train. Within a few months, the legislature was in session, grappling with an enormous fiscal crisis. At the same time, incumbent Mark White and former Governor Bill Clements were gearing up to wage what promised to be a fierce election campaign.

On February 1, a few days after the contract price of West Texas Intermediate Crude was pegged at $25, Mexico slashed its price by $4 per barrel and many other countries also announced substantial reductions. By February 3, spot prices for some grades of crude dropped as low as $17 per barrel and seven-year lows were penetrating the market. In the spirit of Murphy's Law, a series of tornadoes, hail storms, and floods ravaged the Houston area a couple of days later. It seemed again as if even Mother Nature was conspiring against us. About all we were missing was plague and pestilence.

The next week, Venezuela dropped its price to $14.30 and, like many other countries, soon followed with a suspension of any efforts to support its prices in a market bent on driving them down. Throughout this period, West Texas contracts were plummeting, and the specter of a state revenue crunch was looming ever more ominously on the horizon. On February 20, the spot market plunged to $14.17; the next day the $14 threshold was broken. By the end of the month, prices had fallen below $13. By March 5, both the $12 and $11 barriers were shattered. (Perhaps a brief primer on oil prices is in order here. Contract prices are stated in written agreements between refiners and crude suppliers; spot prices reflect an open market transaction for short-term purchases and sales; futures prices are for delivery at a specified date a few weeks or months later. Spot and futures prices generally fluctuate more on a day-to-day basis that the posted contract prices, thus giving a better fix on the all-important issue of what people think.)

In the grand tradition of "it ain't over 'til it's over," the folks in our giant Gulf Coast metropolis launched a "Houston Proud" marketing and civic boosterism campaign smack in the midst of the February oil price avalanche. This effort represented an overt attempt to put Ray's Law of Economics into action. Perception is often a precursor to reality, and the people of Houston wanted to do something about what people think. I realize that I've said so much about my little Law by now that you're probably sick of it, but I can't emphasize enough the extent to which this simple dictum dominates all aspects of economic life.

In a nutshell, this "Houston Proud" campaign was aimed at sparking a unified effort by the area's 3.6 million residents to "sell" the place they called home as a desirable one in which to live and work. By encouraging Houstonians to adopt a "think positive" attitude and to spread that gospel even in the face of adversity, that effort did a lot to restore local confidence and even inspired some new initiatives. In an amazingly short time (less than a year), I would be projecting that Houston would lead the major Texas cities into economic recovery. Although that notion seemed farfetched to others, it turned out that I was right. Rising exports, new petrochemical facilities, expanding consumer electronics manufacturing, and a vibrant health care industry would lead this upswing. Thanks to "Houston Proud," people were more cognizant of the turnaround, and investment money poured in a lot faster than it would have otherwise. By 1988, I would be touting Houston's impressive job growth statistics in speeches around the country. Chalk up another one for what people think.

In February and March of 1986, however, things certainly weren't so upbeat and, rhetoric aside, the economic fortunes of Texas were dominated by daily events. In February, I ventured out to Midland to give a speech about our assessment of what was in store for that metropolitan area in the wake of collapsing oil prices. There's not much out there that isn't tied to petroleum, so it certainly wasn't a bed of roses. My primary recollection of that journey is the fact that I was forced to tell a group of desperate oil folks that I opposed the oil import fees that most Texas politicians in both parties were trying to sell in Washington.

I think just about any attempt to impede the flow of goods and services through the economy will ultimately work to our detriment. If we did manage to pass some sort of fee on oil, we would just be putting off the inevitable and inviting retaliation as we tried to sell our stuff abroad. As far as I was concerned, we needed to find solutions to our economic problems through diversification, not by putting our heads in the sand. The days of building economies exclusively off the land were over, and we had just as well face up to it and get on with some real progress.

That's big talk coming from a short kid with a glass jaw, and I would have been just as happy if that question about my opinion on oil import fees had not come from the floor. I had no idea what the reception would be, but I wasn't expecting the keys to the city. Actually, I was pleasantly surprised. Everybody that came up afterwards said they appreciated my honesty and having the guts to say it. An amazing number of them even said they agreed with me. Putting a bandaid on a rapidly spreading cancer doesn't appeal to a whole lot of Texans when they stop and think about it.

Meanwhile, back at the ranch, the Pennzoil-Texaco saga was alive and well. Still reeling from the stunning verdict, Texaco's lawyers requested a new trial in their ongoing multibillion dollar dispute with Pennzoil in February. The motion was denied, and the next round of the battle began over the bond to be posted by Texaco during the appeals process. When you're talking about more than $10 billion, even the most routine matters can become major issues.

The signs of economic difficulty continued to crop up as Texas struggled through the initial quarter of its sesquicentennial year. Our 150th anniversary, marking the formation of a poor, struggling republic out of what was formerly Mexican territory, was supposed to be a celebration of all that was right with the world. Trail rides, street dances, fireworks displays, armadillo races, music extravaganzas, picnics, black-tie galas, academic convocations, chili cook-offs, and countless other manifestations of Texana came off as scheduled. Texans will rarely let anything interfere with a good party. But the anatomy of the situation was all wrong. We were supposed to have our heads held high while putting our best foot forward. Instead, we were keeping stiff upper lips while frantically covering our backsides.

We have traditionally been a state of legends, tall tales, and exaggeration. From Pecos Bill lassoing a Texas tornado to "One Riot, One Ranger" to Judge Roy Bean meting out his own brand of justice as the "Law West of the Pecos," we have always spun such yarns. Most of them have at least some reasonable combination of fact and fiction, although I doubt that ol' Bill roped anything more than a small West Texas dust storm. I have always attributed this braggadocio to the fact that we were large geographically, had a frontier heritage, and were the only state that was once a separate and independent nation. I heard an interesting alternative theory, however, that carries this Texas trait much farther back into our history. The source was none other than the late John Henry Faulk, the noted humorist and philosopher from Madisonville who certainly qualifies as a genuine Texas legend for whom there is no reason to resort to fiction. He is one of the most interesting and thought-provoking people I've ever met, with a life story that is truly inspirational.

John Henry once told me that the father of Texas brag was none other than Spanish explorer Alvar Nuñez Cabeza de Vaca. He spent several years in Texas in the early 1500s. He roamed around rugged territory, almost starved to death, and was captured by the cannibalistic Karankawa Indians that then inhabited a good portion of the lands that now comprise Texas. Despite his meager existence and experiences that would leave any sane human being reeling in abject terror, he reported back to his Spanish rulers that he had found Seven Cities of Gold. According to John Henry, that was the first Texas tall tale, and we've been telling them ever since. Who am I to argue with him?

Whatever the source, native Texans hear these stories from birth and grow up thinking of ourselves as somehow larger than life and invulnerable. The 1970s only reinforced this phenomenon. As our celebration of all things Texan was getting underway in 1986, though, we were discovering all too graphically our role as one of many participants in a global economic environment. We were subject to cyclical declines and were linked to world events far beyond our control just like everybody else.

When the February unemployment statistics were released, the rate had spurted to 8.8%, a level Texas had not reached since the trough of the prior downturn in early 1983. The jobless percentage tied the highest since records had been kept, but this recession was not your basic garden variety of economic chaos and calamity. Within four months, the unemployment rate would rise to 11.1%. More than one out of ten Texans who wanted to work would be pounding the pavement. Lest we forget, to be classified as unemployed for counting purposes, you must be actively seeking a job. Those who give up and go home are not included. Even by this standard, there were more than 900,000 of us looking for a chance to earn a living in June, 1986. Any way you cut it, that's 4.5 Alaskas without even including the poor folks who got discouraged or just plain fed up and quit trying. Before May of 1986, we had never seen unemployment rates above 9%; once they got here, they decided to stay around for a while. Workers were dropping like flies in all walks of life, although the initial concentrations were among the well-compensated and highly skilled workers in the extraction and related manufacturing industries.

During the first half of March, the contract price of West Texas Crude dropped as low as $14 a barrel. Lone Star Steel, which epitomized the oil-related Texas manufacturing industry, announced new massive layoffs, following the gradual clampdowns the company had already imposed. Lone Star is a large fabricator of pipe and materials headquartered near Daingerfield, a small East Texas town in Morris County. This whole county had once been an exemplary testimony to the prosperity that was Texas during the oil boom. Daingerfield also had a heritage of great high school football teams. In 1986, its unemployment rate soared (or soured) to well above 30%. The number of housing permits in the area literally fell to zero over an extended period. When we were working in 1989 with a major corporate client on some issues regarding development in Morris County, the local folks would trot our real estate people out to see the one house that had been started in the past three years. It was more than a little sad. But even that single modest edifice was a symbol of hope and optimism for the future in the aftermath of the oil price collapse.

In the course of my consulting, I've worked with many communities in East Texas, South Texas, West Texas, and elsewhere that have suffered through similar severe situations. It is very gratifying today, in the early 1990s, to witness some of the results that the hard work and persistence on the part of local citizens have brought about. The fruits of their business development labors have ripened into new jobs and other important economic initiatives.

But in 1986, many regions were in the depths of a major recession. At about the same time as Lone Star Steel was going through another round of cutbacks, Myerland Plaza was posted for foreclosure. This mall, an ancient one by Texas standards, is something of a Houston landmark. It also happens to be a place where I spent a few hours during my graduate school days at Rice University as the oil boom was just getting cranked up (1974-1977).

Because it was older than some, I could find things there that suited my poor student budget a little better that the stuff at the glitzy new centers.

As this seemingly endless first quarter was finally winding down, the OPEC ministers were assembling again in an attempt to stabilize oil markets and prevent additional price collapses. As had become typical, the various competing interests could not be satisfactorily resolved at this meeting. There were, however, modest market rallies from time to time, primarily based on reports of low home heating oil inventories. Such news was only a minor blip, given the overall catastrophe affecting the Texas economy. Several major oil companies, including Exxon and Chevron, were in the process of again slashing their drilling and exploration budgets, this time by as much as 50%. The search for new oil was simply not economically feasible in an environment of excess supplies and falling prices. The market did show some strength over the next few months, as our "year of discontent" continued to march forward, but it did little to stem the tide of our rising problems in other seas.

On another major front, the real estate calamity was creeping up on us. News was beginning to surface regarding the excess supplies of various types of space and falling rental rates and values in the major cities in Texas. Some of the proposed provisions being debated for the new, so-called "Tax Simplification Act" were also causing some of us a great deal of concern. At that point, however, it was far too early to tell what was going to happen. (By the way, if any of you found your taxes simpler as a result of that bill, please let me know.)

Although many banks still appeared to be flourishing, there were increasing signs of trouble. It may be difficult to believe from our current perspective, but in April of 1986, people in Texas considered the declared insolvency of Mainland Savings of Houston to be a very big deal. At the time, with assets of slightly over $1 billion, it was by far the largest such institution ever closed by thrift regulators. It had only been a very short while ago that a commercial had run nationally touting the fact that not one single penny had ever been lost in a savings and loan. A few years later, the remaining price tag on the bailout from a disastrous real estate debacle would be approaching half a trillion dollars.

In April, Farah, a large clothing manufacturer, announced the closing of its plant in El Paso, thus idling 1,000 workers. While this one was certainly larger than most, other manufacturing and distribution facilities for jeans, boots, hats, and bandanas were pulling up the rug on a widespread basis. Our blind presumption that the euphoria over Texas would continue forever had led us to create substantial excess capacity in producing these sorts of goods. The ol' boys in Texas couldn't begin to buy all of that stuff, particularly now that a whole lot of them were out of a job. The Texas boutiques around the country had long since given way to chains, spikes, punk clothes, and whatever else made the cash register ring. The era of emulating Texas oil men had turned into one of ridiculing or maybe even pitying them. The fickle fads of fashion had quickly moved on to other arenas. Texas was out. There is nothing chic about an economy on the skids.

By May, the total U.S. rig count stood at only 809 operating facilities, the lowest level since World War II. Less than five years earlier, Texas alone had more than 1,400 rigs in operation. Even as late as January of 1985, only a little over a year earlier, the state total had exceeded the current level for the nation as a whole. In June, the Texas rig count plummeted to only 216, only about one-seventh of the peak and the lowest level since statewide records had been compiled. (We began keeping a fairly accurate count in the 1940s.) Things were definitely not well in the oil patch. There was one bright note, however. The price of oil did reach a three-month high of $17 per barrel on the open market during the middle of May. But that uptick didn't really change the fundamentals. We were realizing, some of us faster than others, that Texas could no longer depend on oil prices as the main life preserver to keep us afloat. The deaf ears to any talk about diversification in the early 1980s were now perked up and ready to listen.

Texas legislators were faced, as I said earlier, with the sobering recognition that they were going to have to deal with a major budgetary crisis during the midst of an election campaign. The Texas Poll, an opinion survey periodically released within the state, revealed in June that citizens would prefer a tax increase rather than suffer significant reductions in state and local services. That notion certainly had a modicum of logical appeal, particularly since Texas has never been known as a state that spent a great deal on public initiatives and social programs in comparison with other regions. There just wasn't much to cut. Nevertheless, it is a well known dictum in this state that, whatever folks may say to a pleasant voice asking questions over the telephone, Texans still have a mighty aversion to taxes.

Texas as a whole still hangs on to Populist notions about big government being bad. Period. We routinely turn down pay raises for our elected officials. Our constitution has to be amended for what are generally regarded as routine legislative matters in most states. We use it to keep a tight reign on just what the public sector can do without first consulting us. We cling to biennial regular legislative sessions, although, in reality, we find ourselves in numerous special sessions each year. For an awful lot of people in this state, the only good legislative session is one where there are no new taxes. In essence, it's successful if there is not a tax increase and unsuccessful if there is, and they really don't want to hear any more about it.

At any rate, bolstered by the results of the Texas Poll, Governor White ran a campaign in which he openly said that the state required new taxes. By that time, he had earned a reputation as "Media Mark" and was often criticized for changing his stance with each new public opinion survey. For his part, former Governor Clements ran a campaign in which he pledged no new taxes. Virtually everyone knew that he was talking out of the side of his mouth, and that increased levies were inevitable, but voters like to hear it nonetheless. A few years later, we would be reading George Bush's lips in the same way.

The other interesting claim by Bill Clements during the race was, in essence, that oil prices had nothing to do with the problems in Texas, the implication being that it was all Mark White's fault. He pointed out that average prices were higher in his opponent's term (1983-1986) than they had been in his prior tenure (1979-1982). About all you can get out of that one is that you shouldn't pay too much attention to averages. Prices were shooting up during the oil boom. They got to a peak and fell. It looked sort of like an upside-down "V." The averages were about the same, but how you got there was altogether different. A lot of Texas graphs looked like upside-down V's in those days. Clements caught 'em going up; White endured 'em coming down.

Whatever the reason, the "workhorse" beat the "showhorse," and Texans swept the former governor back into office. As we all know, Governor Clements ultimately approved the largest tax hikes in Texas history. I suppose one lesson to be learned from all of this is that, if you are going to seek political office in Texas, don't advocate new taxes, even if you know they're inevitable. The other lesson is that, if you want to be re-elected, don't be governor during an oil bust. (One of the major factors that led to the defeat of Governor Clements in 1982 had been the first oil glut.)

In July, another giant corporation hit the ropes. In the continuing saga of LTV, this ultimate symbol of the era of conglomerates filed for Chapter 11 bankruptcy protection. The lawyers were also busy filing all sorts of complicated papers in the Pennzoil-Texaco fracas.

That summer, OPEC members agreed upon some production cuts, but nothing on the magnitude that would restore the oil market to anything close to its former luster. In Texas, the special sessions to deal with the fiscal crisis were very intense during the summer and fall of 1986. Both interstate and branch banking were approved for the state in one sweep in late August. More than a century of Texas tradition—of the sovereignty of independent banks and the sanctity of Texas-owned institutions—gave way to the march of time and the exigencies of competitiveness. Maybe more important, from the point of view of the Texas lawmakers who cast the "yes" votes to break down the barriers of this long tradition, was the fact that such a move was, whether they liked it or not, an absolute necessity.

The state banking system had long lagged those in other parts of the country in moving to take advantage of economies of scale and access to capital. The same Populist traditions that held government in check embodied a healthy distrust of large concentrations of financial power as well. Texas has been an importer of funds since its days as a republic and has suffered through more than one currency crisis.

During the oil boom, our banks had been ranked among the best in the country both in terms of growth and profitability. By 1986, however, we had reached a point where the very survival of our banking system depended on cutting costs and acquiring new infusions of funds. As the remainder of the 1980s played out, branch banking and purchases of Texas banks by out-of-state institutions would become a normal course of business and one of the keys to our "survival" in this most difficult decade. At the time, however, it was one more blow to the Texas mystique, sort of like outlawing snuff or pickup trucks.

In the fall of '86, the market reaction to some of OPEC's production cuts began to take hold, and there were modest oil price increases. The economic difficulties were only beginning, however. The level of drilling activity in the Gulf of Mexico reached historic lows, with only 71 rigs in operation. Energy companies continued to announce layoffs, new real estate information was less than encouraging, and the budgetary crisis loomed ever larger.

Concerns about the new federal tax laws that were going into effect the next year were also well justified. The capacity to sell real estate at reduced prices was largely fueled by well-to-do people with very high earning streams from other sources, such as doctors and lawyers, who needed tax write-offs. Under traditional tax policy, these folks could buy real estate at reduced prices and incur "paper losses" (depreciation and such). These "losses" could then be used to offset their relatively high earned incomes when it came time to write the check to the Internal Revenue Service. The real kicker was that, when real estate values came back a few years later, they could sell the stuff at a big profit and only pay the relatively low long-term capital gains tax rates on the deal. The new tax law blew the lid off of this little trick and took these buyers out of the market. Believe me, there were very few others.

This law also killed the oil and gas tax shelter game; but, by 1986, the market had pretty much taken care of that anyway. By segmenting income into active, passive, and portfolio categories and not letting you mix them up, the new tax code eliminated the opportunity for high income individuals to achieve tax advantages through investments such as real estate, oil wells, Arabian horses, and registered bulls. With no buyers in the market, the capacity of the financial sector to sustain its large real estate portfolios simply wasn't there. The legislation also changed some of the direct accounting practices of banks in ways that were not favorable to the old after-tax bottom line. Many financial institutions had to bite the bullet and admit that they were holding a train load of not-so-valuable real estate loans that were getting even less valuable by the day. The "write-down" process was arduous. It required massive capital infusions, or, in many cases when the money just flat wasn't there, led to deliberate reductions in size or turning in the keys to the Feds.

Now I am definitely not an accountant (I don't have the personality), but I'll try to explain this process as best I can. Banks, like all businesses, have assets, liabilities, and capital. Assets are things like loans and government securities. Liabilities are primarily deposits, that is, my money and your money. The capital stock is what the owners have, or the net worth of the bank.

Two simple rules come into play here. One of them is the basic accounting identity, which says that assets have to add up to liabilities plus capital. That one is fundamental; you just can't get away from it. It's kind of like Ray's Law of Economics.

The other rule is a government regulation that says a bank's capital has to be a certain percent of its assets. This requirement is supposed to be a source of comfort and protection for depositors. The formulas to calculate the needed amount of capital have been evolving since the Great Depression, so they are fairly complicated. Fortunately, we don't need to worry about the details.

When the value of a loan (or asset) is written down on the books of the bank, it doesn't do anything to deposits. We have the same amount of money in the bank as before. Hence, it comes right out of the capital stock. If you have to lower the value of enough of them, sooner or later your capital is going to get below the required level. At that point, you either have to (1) add more capital, (2) make the bank smaller, so that the capital you have left is enough to meet the guidelines, or (3) shut the doors and go home. End of lesson.

As I have often said over the past few years, almost all of the folks who owned banks in Texas at the time had made their real money in either oil or real estate. Even if they made it in some other way the first time around, they had managed to tie it up in oil and real estate by the mid-1980s. Consequently, when the crunch came, they didn't have anything left to recapitalize their bank with, even if they did, such an investment would not be very high on the old priority list. After all, the title of the part of this book that refers to the 1980s is "survive!" People were looking for oxygen, not caviar.

As per our lesson, a common strategy during this period was for banks to deliberately get smaller. This technique is precisely the sort of thing that an already struggling economy does NOT need, because it means that business loans, not to mention consumer loans, will dry up. Nevertheless, for many financial institutions in Texas, it was the only way to make it. Another approach was to ignore the problem and retain the values of loan portfolios on the books at current values in the hopes that the regulators wouldn't notice and the crisis would pass without incident. They did and it didn't.

Let's look at a few numbers to illustrate this phenomenon. Loans in Texas banks peaked at the end of 1985, totaling about

$123 billion. By the end of the decade, they would be hovering around $80 billion, having dropped by more than one-third. When the overall amount of loans in the books drops by that much, you can bet that almost no new ones are being added. Deposits also topped out in 1985 at about $156 billion and ended the decade at $134 billion. Where I come from, we call that a credit crunch of the first magnitude. When you couple that with the fact that most of the out-of-state lenders were "red-lining" Texas, you end up in a situation where it's real tough to finance a decent economic recovery. (For those of you who are unfamiliar with the term "red-lining," it basically means that, if the loan application was from Texas, it was denied. Period.)

I suppose it is somewhat fitting that the first merger under the new interstate banking law took place between a bank in Texarkana, Texas and one in Texarkana, Arkansas. In old Texas style, we didn't exactly rush out to the East Coast to find our first partner. We wanted to get our feet wet first. It would not be long until New York, California, North Carolina, Illinois, Ohio and others would join the list in earnest. Suitors who had always wanted a crack at the vast Texas market would, with the help of the Feds, be coming at us from all over the map.

Toward the end of the year, a report was released showing declines in the net worth of 70% of savings and loan associations in Texas, but even at this point only half were on the "critical list." By December, it appeared as if some of the general Texas turmoil was settling down to some extent. OPEC had agreed to 5% production cuts across the board and Boone Pickens was making yet another takeover run, this time in hot pursuit of Diamond Shamrock. On the downside, LTV had lost more than $3 billion during the year, and the number of bank failures in the state had more than doubled. During 1987, we would see the final playout of the Pennzoil-Texaco court battles, an intense legislative session dealing with budgetary issues, and the initial effects of the new tax legislation on real estate markets. On the national front, the stock market would be good for a few magic moments.

All in all, 1986 ended much more quietly than it began. It was the kind of year that no one predicts and no one is prepared for. It was full of mixed signals. It was a time when Texas celebrated its 150th birthday and mourned the loss of hundreds of thousands of jobs. From the peak of this cycle in late 1985 to the trough in early 1987, more than 260,000 jobs were lost. As with any year, there were bright spots. Gruman announced a major move of its facilities to Houston, and IBM began construction of a major new complex in the Dallas/Fort Worth Metroplex. On the whole, however, it was a time that we would just as soon forget.

As an economist and unabashed Texas booster, I saw a few silver linings in the generally cloudy coming year. The world economic situation was becoming ripe for expansion of export activity, and Texas would be a major player in this resurgence. The dollar was down, foreigners were buying, and we stood ready to ship to them. Lower oil prices encouraged the consumption of petrochemicals, and capacity constraints made investment in new facilities appear feasible. Our excess commercial real estate space and relatively cheap land and labor costs, which were to some extent the by-products of our recession, also helped to make Texas more attractive and would give us a tremendous advantage in recruiting major new facilities over the next few years. I had the privilege of being involved in many opportunities to illustrate this concept and, thus, help bring new business to the state during the final phase of the 1980s.

One particularly gratifying aspect of the expanding export potential was that it could potentially help the farmers of the state. As a country boy from East Texas, I have a special place in my heart for all of them. The best days of my youth were spent on my Pop's (my maternal grandfather) farm in Red Springs, Texas. (For those of you who don't know, that's over close to Sand Flat and not too far from Winona.) In my capacity as an economic consultant, I've worked very closely with rural communities, suppliers of electricity and telephone service to rural areas, and other groups interested in preserving this important part of Texas heritage. One of the silent tragedies of 1986 was the fact that farmers were dropping like flies. The combination of falling land values, difficulties in obtaining financing, high debt service cost, falling mineral values, regulation, droughts, floods, and freezes was taking its toll. When you added to that the "brain drain" and falling population in many rural counties, the situation really looked tough.

It turned out that we were losing 113 farmers and ranchers a week during 1985. By 1986, Texas farmers were battling their worst economic odds in half a century, and it looked like 10,000 of them might be forced to quit within the year. This important export sector of Texas was in significant need of revitalization.

As usual, when I saw a sinking ship, I jumped in and grabbed a bucket. I would soon find myself as the primary spokesperson for an initiative to promote agricultural processing in Texas. I also worked to insure adequate electricity supplies at reasonable prices, state-of-the-art telephone service, and sufficient water for agricultural needs. All of this activity was part of my ongoing effort to assist the farmers and their communities in Texas, and I look forward to even further activity of this nature as we move into the 1990s.

As 1985 had been, 1987 was in many ways a year of transition. After the wholesale carnage of the past year, we definitely needed one. The trough in our employment hit early in the year; we then started the slow climb back up the hill. From the beginning of 1987 to the end of 1989, the state would gain more than 450,000 jobs (about 2.3 Alaskas). While it would have been premature to claim that a full-fledged recovery was starting early in the year, it was clearly in progress a few months later. Unfortunately, however, no one seemed to notice.

One more time, Texas found itself in an unfortunate situation where perceptions and reality were out of sync. The most important thing is what people think, and people had a lot of opportunities to think bad things about Texas in 1987. Everything you read about sounded awful. Press reports were full of downers. There were stories about the record number of bankruptcies, foreclosures, bank failures, and all the other negative situations that had occurred in the state. Governor Connally, Lieutenant Governor Barnes, and their joint real estate venture all filed bankruptcy during the year. There was even one article about the pluggers who were going all across West Texas putting the lid on once active oil wells. The headline on that story was "The Undertakers of the Oil Patch." That's not exactly the sort of thing the local chamber of commerce would pick for the cover of a brochure.

The fact that Texas had a recession while the rest of the nation enjoyed prosperity was on the minds of everyone. It was certainly a turnaround from the 1970s and early 1980s. The jokes about the oil patch were rampant throughout the country. Things were so bad in Louisiana that the Mafia had to lay off six judges. Pigeons were the only ones in Midland who could leave a deposit on a Mercedes. The only way to get a Texas banker out of a tree was to cut the rope . . . And on and on and on.

When the state fell on bad times, Texas bashing became the order of the day. After all, folks hadn't forgotten that old bumper sticker. Disturbing real estate statistics were being released as fast as somebody could grind them out. Prominent Texans were finding their personal financial problems making headlines throughout the country. Bank earnings reports were less than encouraging. The legislature was grappling, in open sessions, with a major budgetary crisis. Indeed, there was plenty to write about when it came to Texas. While most of the stories were really focusing on the workout of old problems as the economy was beginning to reactivate, that small subtlety was quickly washed away in a sea of notable negatives.

Just to keep you posted, an appeals court issued a ruling favoring Pennzoil in its ongoing battle with Texaco over the purchase of Getty Oil. With accumulated interest, the tab in that historic judgment now exceeded $11 billion. In April, Texaco filed for Chapter 11 protection as a device to prevent (or, at least, stall) the enforcement of the court mandate. Pennzoil kept wanting to put up those yellow signs, but Texaco was still partial to black and red.

Around mid-year, the two giants of Dallas banking, InterFirst and Republic, merged their organizations into First RepublicBank. They had been discussing the possibility of a merger off and on for about a year and had announced their plans the previous December. They had finally finished the process of dotting the *i*'s, crossing the *t*'s, and making the regulators happy. A lot of the Texas banks were putting aside substantial loan loss reserves at this time and were feeling the crunch of the energy and real estate situation. Nonetheless, a great deal of hope accompanied this merger.

InterFirst had been an aggressive oil and gas lender, and had been among the first of the large Texas banks to experience substantial problems. Rumors about its future had been swirling all over the place. Republic had taken a much more conservative approach in its energy portfolio. The merger brought opportunities for considerably greater efficiency in the Texas banking situation. A lot of operations could be streamlined and consolidated, and the banks in many local markets were combined into branches. Selfishly, many Texans liked the fact that it kept a big bank, our biggest, in local hands. We still like things "home grown."

During this year of the breather, the initial load of fuel went to the South Texas project (STP), the large nuclear plant that had broken ground in the early 1970s in the midst of an "oil boom." At the time, given the rapidly escalating gas prices and extremely healthy economy, a nuclear energy source was believed to be essential to the future of the Texas Gulf Coast. But necessity can be a relative thing, especially when the whole economic universe changes. This plant, along with Comanche Peak in North Texas, had a history of lengthy delays and cost overruns. Both plants were also completed in much more sluggish business environments than the ones they faced on groundbreaking day. Nonetheless, they are massive and impressive facilities and will, despite all the controversy surrounding them, be vitally important to the infrastructure of Texas in the long run. Only a few months after the fuel loading began, I found myself immersed in the regulatory hearings related to the rate increases required to fund the cost of participation in STP in a fair and equitable manner. Another reason why the reports about Texas continued to reflect negativism, despite job growth throughout most of the year, was the unevenness of the economic situation. President Eisenhower would have probably called it a "rolling readjustment." Cities like Houston, which were intimately connected to world oil markets, felt the initial brunt of the oil shock in 1986. Houston was hit earlier and harder. I have often said that if the price of oil started falling at 9:00 in the morning, layoffs would begin on the Gulf Coast by noon. While the response is not quite that immediate, it is indeed rapid, substantial, and intense. On the other hand, Houston moved into the recovery a lot quicker than most, avoiding at least some of the worst of the S&L fallout.

By 1987, some of the other metropolitan areas in Texas were experiencing regional difficulties which were masked in the aggregate numbers for the state. Take Dallas, for instance. As a center for trade, transportation, communications, finance, and other activities, Dallas is one of the major urban hubs of the nation. The impacts of oil price shocks are felt later in Dallas, well after they've touched down in places such as East Texas, West Texas, Oklahoma, and Louisiana. When the retailers from these oil producing areas come to Dallas for market, they don't buy nearly as much stuff as they would if the rigs were working. When notes from the oil folks become due, they have to be restructured and extended, thus stretching the earnings of the financial institutions. When business is slow, people don't travel as much. All of these factors combine to bring slowdowns in business activity to areas such as Dallas several months after the slide in the regions where the petroleum industry plays a more direct role in the economy. Because Dallas had been more prosperous than Houston during the real estate frenzy, it had bigger problems to deal with in 1987. Construction employment was really falling like a bucket of cement from the top of one of those recently completed skyscrapers.

It was also during this period that there was another fairly major glut in the world market for a number of electronic components, many of which were manufactured in Texas. So our high tech industry was hit, too. Electronics is a great industry to have, but it is cyclical. This excess supply situation led to layoffs in both Austin and the Metroplex. Austin saw its technology work force shrink by about 5% in a single year. Additionally, because of the glamour and attention attached to electronic bells and whistles, the state capitol had been the most visible center of excessive real estate development in the entire country. As that activity cratered, Austin went into its downturn. In other words, while the state as a whole saw job growth in 1987, it was not a case of balanced expansion across the board. Some areas were gaining and some were losing. When I went to give a speech in Dallas or Austin about our economic situation, there was no point in talking about our modest, tentative statewide recovery. The folks in those areas just weren't seeing it.

Among the positive notes for the year were the opening of the Hardy Toll Road in Houston and the major corporate relocation of retailing giant J.C. Penney from New York City to Plano. During 1987, Southwestern Bell purchased Metromedia, a further indication of the new environment surrounding the divested telecommunications industry in which more and more facets were becoming competitive. The legislature also enacted some significant economic development initiatives, including the creation of a state Department of Commerce. I had been privileged to serve on a task force appointed by House Speaker Gib Lewis which recommended many of the new programs. It didn't bring us up to the level of some of our competitors, but at least it was a good start.

My star was also rising a little higher beyond Texas. The stock market had crashed in October, and the forecasting community was dutifully falling in line to predict that a national recession would happen six months later. That's the way it always happened. On the day after all the commotion, however, I released a report that said just the opposite. We projected that, if anything, the U.S. would expand even more than had been anticipated previously. As

I saw it, all of the forces that were driving this particular expansion were either left alone or reinforced by what was going on in the market.

It's not enough to just know what's occurred in the past. You have to understand why. Forecasters must analyze a situation in light of the past, but keep any eye on what is similar and what is not. Otherwise, we won't do any better than a simple trend line. We have to study all relevant phenomena intensely. Nobody who prognosticates about the business world is going to be right all of the time. There are just too many things that can blindside us. I've often said that there are only three types of forecasters—the new, the humble, and the former. I've been around awhile, and I'm still here. That pretty well puts me in the middle group.

Providing economic projections is not like taking an exam from one of those wonderful professors who asks the same questions semester after semester (they were always my favorites). You can't just go to file, get the test, and memorize the old answers. You have to do your homework. In any case, my national outlook in October of 1987, and an earlier one in which I bolted from the crowd and nailed some interest rate movements, at least let folks know that you don't have to be in New York to figure out what's going on. Texans have been looking at horseshoes for years.

Shortly after Thanksgiving, the Supreme Court of Texas failed to take any action to change the judgment in the Pennzoil-Texaco case and the legal scramble intensified. Texaco sought mechanisms to move the agenda to federal court, while settlement talks picked up steam. By the end of the year, the parties agreed upon a $3 billion settlement. Once again, the record books were rewritten.

It was also about this time, near the end of the year, that I joined with a few friends and colleagues to begin speculating on some straightforward mechanisms to deal with and try to avert what, in my simple mind, was already shaping up to be a crisis that would cost hundreds of billions of dollars and would affect the entire nation. I'm talking, of course, about the S&L fiasco and the general cleanup of the financial and real estate situation in Texas and, indeed, the entire country.

One idea that came immediately to mind was to put a "grandfather clause" in that notorious Tax Simplification Act. Basically, the amendment would allow projects that existed prior to 1987 to be exempt from active and passive income separation and other onerous provisions. The original law that contributed to the building binge clearly needed to be changed. I had been saying that for years. It convinced people to build space for tax purposes, rather than because the economy needed it. The new problem was that we changed horses in the middle of the stream. The changes in tax breaks for real estate, without a safety valve for existing properties, had the effect of saying that, since tax policy had been the initial culprit, we certainly wanted to make sure that it didn't have a chance to be an effective part of the solution. It's sort of like teaching a child that if they do something wrong, they should never, ever try to make amends for it. It doesn't make a whole lot of sense, but we are talking about Washington, D.C. here.

If we had permitted a grandfather clause, it would have raised the after-tax rate of return on existing projects enormously, and the private sector would have taken it from there. It would have cost a few billion dollars in revenue at the time, but it might have saved a few *hundred* billion dollars in expenditures and taxes a little farther on down the road.

The other principal idea that we kicked around was a plan in which institutions could swap real estate assets for bonds backed by the land, shopping malls, mini-storage buildings, and see-through office complexes that were in the ailing portfolios. The details are fairly complicated, but the notion was to get the real estate off the books, so the institutions could get back into the business of lending money and out of the business of managing property. The concept was fairly simple for someone from the country: We have too much of the stuff, so let's build a big warehouse to put it in until we need it. (It was kind of like the potato shed on my Pop's farm.) The only difference is that, instead of bricks and mortar, this warehouse would be built out of pieces of paper. The idea was akin to the old Reconstruction Finance Corporation that was created in 1932 as a mechanism to help bring the country out of the Great Depression.

It was difficult to build a constituency for a comprehensive program at that point. Part of the dilemma was that Congress would have been admitting that they had really messed up in the first place. They don't like to do that. The bigger difficulty with any agenda was that many influential people continued to view the calamity in the financial sector as a localized "Texas problem." There was that bumper sticker, you know.

The year, as I've said, had more than its share of bad news about the financial and real estate sectors, including a pronouncement by Governor Clements that depositors in thrift institutions might receive only 30¢ on the dollar. In the environment of the times, that was not the most encouraging of statements. The nation would have to come to grips with this massive problem over the next few years and I would end up on a lot of special committees, task forces, and witness stands before all was said and done. For now, however, it was viewed more as a Texas problem or, seen in the greatest of largesse, as a situation that could be solved by "The Southwest Plan." That "Plan" was the controversial program instituted by the Federal Savings and Loan Insurance Corporation (FSLIC) in 1988 in which eighty-seven broke thrifts were merged into fifteen larger institutions. Then, sweetened with huge tax breaks and promises of continued federal subsidies, the government put these newly combined entities up for sale. One quote that came back to haunt me occurred when I was first asked to publicly comment on the Southwest Plan. I said, "It's kind of like rearranging the deck chairs on the Titanic. It looks a little better, but the ship's still sinking!" A lot of folks didn't appreciate that one, but history has already shown it to be correct. I call 'em like I see 'em. What can I say?

NINE

The Real Recovery

NOW YOU DON'T SEE IT, NOW YOU DO: 1988 AND 1989

The year 1988 was a strange one. I call it the year of the invisible recovery. In 1987, we hit bottom from the devastation of the 1986 shipwreck, and began to get our sea legs again. The comeback was tentative and uneven. By 1989, we were really in an all-out recovery and people had started to sit up and take notice. The year in the middle was 1988. What else can I say? During that year, Texas indeed made some impressive gains. The numbers were up on all sorts of economic barometers: jobs, output, income, sales, and just about any other indicator you'd care to look at, or hear about, or smell.

By September, we had regained all of the jobs we had lost in the terrible torrent of terror that accompanied the oil market catastrophe. For the first ten months of the year, however, it was the bad news—more big bank failures, personal bankruptcies, and real estate foreclosures—that grabbed the lion's share of the headlines and dominated conversations at luncheon meetings, golf courses, and cocktail parties. The data may have been improving, but the bombardment with negativism was continuing to make us feel even worse. More important was the fact that the perpetual flood of adverse publicity around the globe affected attitudes about Texas in national and international markets. In other words (you guessed it), it affected what people think. I found myself talking to New York bond raters, German bankers, Swiss insurers, Japanese investors, and a whole boatload of other folks from all parts of creation. It remained hard to get loans made, bonds sold, and deals done when people still thought we were drowning in our own misery. (Somehow, we managed.)

My own year got off to a less than auspicious start. In January, *Texas Monthly* heaped their not-so-coveted Bum Steer Award upon me. We had been tracking U-Haul patterns as part of a study on population migration in the state and published the results in one of our newsletters. (Our economic newsletter, modestly titled *The Perryman Report*, now enjoys a monthly circulation of several thousand, a far cry from the six good folks who received my first forecast.) What we uncovered in our investigation was the fact that people were moving from Houston to Austin/San Antonio, Austin/San Antonio to Dallas, and Dallas to Houston. We were chasing our tails, it seems. As the bearer of this message, I got a Bum Steer from the feisty monthly magazine that is so totally irreverent, Texas style (I love it!). Actually, I suppose it is more accurate to say that I accepted my "award" on behalf of the mobile population of Texas.

About a month before I was given this lofty prize, I had ventured over to Amsterdam to be honored as the Outstanding Young Person in the World in the Field of Business and Economic Innovation. Several thousand people watched as a beautiful trophy was handed to me by John Naisbitt, whose writings on the American business and political life have literally changed our vocabulary. (He and I had worked together a year or so earlier on an economic development program in Central Texas.) That award was one of a string of commendations I've received for my academic and "real world" endeavors related to the use of information to solve economic problems, mostly in Texas. I'm not sure how all of that happened, or how so many people found out about it. I basically just get up every morning (usually I never went to bed in the first place) and do whatever looks like it needs to be done that day to keep the old ball rolling. It really hasn't changed all that much over the years. I'm real glad to be here, although the trophy from Amsterdam and the Bum Steer Award don't exactly make for a matched pair on the shelf.

As 1988 began, there were still many signs of our recent economic annihilation, and that legacy gave more than ample opportunity to write and broadcast bad stuff about Texas. The thing that everyone seemed to forget about the bankruptcies, foreclosures, and other notable negatives is that they did not come from new problems, but were hangovers from the rolling economic collapse which started years earlier. We were basically going uphill by now, but some folks still had to pay the piper (or figure out clever ways to avoid him), particularly on the banking, thrift, and real estate fronts. None of these dates with destiny, however, were the result of things going on in 1988.

Toward the end of January, Houston's Allied Bancshares and California's First Interstate merged as a measure to protect and strengthen the bank group anchored by the largest of Texas' state-chartered banks. They also pulled off one of the fastest statewide sign changes in history. Allied disappeared from the Texas landscape faster than a blue tick hound dog running from a den of stirred up polecats. New York's giant Chemical Bank had already purchased Texas Commerce and had pumped up this oil center bank with a fresh batch of money. This time, though, the signs stayed the same. The major Texas bank holding companies, which had been flying high with soaring stock values in the early 1980s, now found themselves in the uncomfortable position of seeking suitors in order to maintain their solvency.

During the spring of '88, First Republic required substantial infusion of funds from the Federal Deposit Insurance Corporation (FDIC), to the tune of $1 billion, just to stay afloat. The federal safety net didn't do the trick. By early May, the bank suspended interest payments on its debt. Not long afterward, in late July, remnants of this merged entity of two once-mighty Texas financial institutions filed for Chapter 11 protection. A few days earlier most of its assets had been acquired by NCNB. The NCNB deal included a pledge to the newly-created NCNB-Texas from the FDIC for about $4 billion and was given some additional support from H. Ross Perot. It seems like almost every time Texas needs a clutch hit, this modern Lone Star legend steps up to the plate. He's just about always good for a sharp line drive up the middle, and has been known to park more than a few of them way up in the center field seats.

The thrifts were really hit hard. Lamar Savings was included among several institutions in a record $2 billion bailout in May. By the end of the year, this record would be broken, and then some, as we faced the inevitable consequences of the excessive lending from the early part of the decade.

My attentions were focused on banking and real estate in a significant way during this time. In addition to a lot of consulting on the subject, I was involved in five or six efforts to get something done. I'll mention a couple of them. A group of us working under the auspices of State Representative Bruce Gibson, Chairman of the House Banking Committee in Texas, formed a task force to look at possible alternatives for "warehousing" the excess real estate supplies through a bonding program. This particular variation on the notion that I discussed earlier was directed primarily to some of the smaller institutions that were being thrown out with an ocean of dirty bath water.

At the same time, I was meeting with some individuals on a regular basis who were working at the federal level on a much broader initiative. This self-appointed SWAT team included, at various times, the likes of Walt Rostow, a noted economic thinker and writer and advisor to President Lyndon Johnson; the senior leadership of the regional regulatory institutions; and a lot of prominent elected officials and corporate bigwigs. It was spearheaded by Glenn Biggs, himself a legendary Texas business and political leader, who was working, at the request of the FSLIC, on an abortive effort to maintain the viability of Gill Savings in San Antonio. This group agitated at high levels about warehousing programs, the "grandfather clause" concept, and several of the best parts of the current legislation. (The meals were great, too.)

As an aside, a few months later I was asked to speak at the Governor's Conference on Women. I'm not sure why they picked me, but I certainly wasn't going to complain. At any rate, I was introduced by the other half of the Rostow dynamic duo. Elspeth Rostow is a noted scholar and former dean of the Lyndon Baines Johnson School of Public Affairs at the University of Texas. In her remarks that morning, she referred to me as "Walt's Favorite Economist." Those three words meant more to me than all the awards I have ever received. They can carve that one on my tombstone.

As another aside, we can finally close the book on the continuing soap opera feud between Pennzoil and Texaco. In the final episode, Texaco emerged from its self-imposed exile in the warm confines of Chapter 11 in late March of 1988. A couple of weeks later, four checks totalling $3 billion were sent through the Federal Reserve System, which can only process checks of a penny less than $1 billion. This epic struggle generated still another historical footnote. It marked the first time that the country couldn't handle a private transaction with a single check. The Texas justice system scored a victory over the U.S. monetary system. At long last, the apparent deal that was negotiated between Pennzoil and Getty in the waning days of 1984 had come full circle. Mercifully, the preoccupation of the world with this whole mess could finally be put to bed.

The financial falls from grace were not all within the rank of banks, oil companies, and big corporations. During the early part of 1988, a few Texas icons also took well-publicized personal tumbles. For one, former Governor John Connally, who was also Secretary of the Treasury in the Nixon Administration, was forced to hold an auction of some of the assets from his estate as part of his bankruptcy workout. In the tradition of great Texans, he held his head high and won the respect of the nation as he dealt with his problems. He also used his charisma and promotional skills to turn the auction into a major Texas happening and, in the process, netted far more funds than anyone thought possible. It is somewhat ironic that the man who was the spokesperson for the program that floated the dollar and took the U.S. off of the gold standard in 1971 lost his own golden touch in the aftermath of his ill-fated real estate investment ventures in Texas. He did not, however, lose his spurs.

Another personal bankruptcy was declared shortly thereafter by world-renowned Houston heart surgeon, Dr. Denton Cooley. I happened to be involved in that one as a consultant to one of Dr. Cooley's major creditors, First City Bank (which, by this time, had obtained its rescue from Chicago investor A. Robert Abboud). I got a chance to look through the various documents that were part of the Reorganization Plan. The thing that absolutely amazed me about this one was just how much money it was possible for a prominent person to borrow in Texas in the mid-'80s for what turned out to be vastly overvalued real estate investment ventures.

In looking back at the real estate development situation now, it is inconceivable that the amount of raw land that was sold at speculative prices in Texas could possibly have been developed profitably in a reasonable period of time, even if the price of oil had risen to $85 in '85. Of course, a whole lot of folks were participating in this process, and nobody was quite sure what everybody else was doing. One building on a corner might have worked, but four wouldn't. In fact, the one guy who was prudent, did his homework, and got to the corner with the first project, would often be taken down right along with the others. Such is the way of the real estate market game played in a lending environment that's out of control.

During the first months of 1988, there were even more statistics released that focused on the bankruptcy and foreclosure problems within the state. They were greeted with another flood of publicity. Throughout all of this notoriety, however, the monthly economic numbers kept getting better and showed that the state was actually gaining momentum in a business upswing that had some genuine staying power.

There were certainly some major high points, even from practically day one of the new year. We didn't waste any time establishing 1988 as a year of destiny. On January 6, it was announced that Sematech, a hot new research and manufacturing consortium for sophisticated electronics, had selected Austin as the site for its new facilities. We had already been bolstered in a more subtle way by the news that a new trade agreement between the United States and Canada would open up significant markets for Texas products. Petrochemical investments were being made in Texas at multibillion dollar levels, and many other good things seemed to be on the horizon.

This was also the year that long-time Senator Lloyd Bentsen, from Mission in the Rio Grande Valley, snagged the number two spot on the Democratic ticket for president. Of course, Texas' own adopted son, George Bush, won an easy delegate majority at the Republican National Convention to head his party's slate. Bentsen and Bush had met before on the political battlefield, in the 1970 Senatorial race in Texas. This time around, though, the winners would be reversed. Still, these quests for the highest and the next-highest office in the land by Texans were unmistakable evidence of an increasing influence in Washington.

Through the year, there were still major ups and downs. A severe drought continued to grip West Texas. By mid-summer, Southmark, a real estate and financial conglomerate based in Dallas, ceased paying corporate dividends. This mixed bag of news items often camouflaged the underlying growth in Texas. With each new statistical release, the evidence of a major improvement in the fortunes of the state was mounting.

It was a frustrating time for many people, both personally and in large and small business settings. Funding for business growth was difficult to obtain, venture capital was even tougher to find, and traditional modes of operating were changing faster than a champion cutting horse could make a turn. Financing based on cost was a thing of the past; everything was driven by cash flow. Handshakes were being replaced by a sea of paperwork, all written in the incomprehensible dialect known as "legalese." More and more often, some of the folks who came to the table called another country "home." New bank owners from other states replaced "Can I he'p ya?" with "How is it that I may be of service in assisting you?" Although we were well past the dawn of a substantial recovery, few could seem to see that Texas was surging forward.

By the end of 1988, my own frustrations were coming to a head as well. I had spent the better part of a year telling people that Texas was recovering. I pointed out that growth was happening, but that the image had not caught up to the reality. Once again, what people think comes into play. We still couldn't get money really flowing into Texas, because the folks who controlled all those dollars, marks, and yen were still reading about how bad things were.

Toward the end of the year, I was asked to write an article for *Business Facilities* magazine describing some of the attractive features of Texas as a site for new industrial locations. I fractured Mark Twain's famous quote for a good cause and splashed big letters across the top of the article that read, "The Rumors of Our Death Have Been Greatly Exaggerated." Patience still isn't one of my stronger virtues.

Just as I was writing this admittedly pro-Texas piece, however, forces were being set in motion which would help turn around the public image of Texas. People, and not just the few of us who were out there shouting good news to deaf ears, were beginning to recognize the viability of what was happening. In November, the big news on the political front, of course, was that Mr. Bush had been elected president, and there was a great deal of talk about Texans who would be in positions of power. Early in that same month, Formosa Plastics, a Taiwanese company, announced that it was about to open a new plant in Point Comfort, near Victoria, that could potentially be the biggest petrochemical facility in Texas history. The initial investment was to be $1.3 billion.

The really super news, from an economic development standpoint for Texas, came on November 10. I have often said that two things happened on that fateful day, one of which got the world really excited. I gave a speech in Midland, and the Department of Energy announced its intention to build the Superconducting Super Collider in Waxahachie, a small community in Ellis County, south of Dallas. The eyes of the world were suddenly focused on an attractive community with a rural heritage located on the fringes of a dynamic metropolitan region.

The Super Collider announcement was indeed a major one. It was the biggie that we needed. This new national research laboratory had been discussed for years and intense competition for the site had been conducted at all levels—political, geological, economic, you name it. Once again the land was good to us, but this time in a totally different way. One of the clinchers in the decision to locate the facility in Waxahachie was the absolute geographic integrity of the land. We may have tornadoes, floods, and droughts, but we don't have earthquakes. So seismic stability became one of our big selling points. I later found out that it had something to do with the fact that three different types of rock formations came together in Ellis County. I have no idea what all of that means, but if it helps, I'll take it.

What was I doing in Midland on a day like this? Why wasn't I down there with the muckity mucks talking about this great big atom smashing hole in the ground? I often skip the fanfare at the end. By then, I'm usually moving on to the next project. I had been shipping numbers to Washington, stumping around the state trying to get bonds approved, and a thousand other things to promote this initiative for years. I would jump back into the fray shortly thereafter, working on funding and as part of the research team working on the master plan for the project. On November 10, however, I had a long-standing commitment to talk to a group of business leaders in Midland about new development initiatives for their area. I felt it was important that I be there.

It was really a fairly typical day for me (to the extent any of my days are typical). I had a breakfast meeting with a group of economists in Dallas, flew to Midland and spoke at lunch, then ventured back to Dallas to meet with a couple of clients and work on several front-burner projects. I did squeeze a few dozen interviews into the agenda. A few days later, GTE announced a major relocation of its corporate facilities to the Dallas area as well. Within a couple of weeks, Fujitsu, a large Japanese telecommunications company, followed suit, heralding the planned move of its

North American manufacturing and research headquarters to Richardson. This combination of events, centered around the magnetic attraction of the Super Collider (pardon still another pun!), suddenly caused people around the globe to sit up and take notice of Texas again in an entirely different and much more positive light. Finally, we were cooking in grease.

In the span of just a month, we had three major corporate locations, a Texan elected President, my speech in Midland, and of course, the Super Collider. Folks were now abuzz with talk of the "Great Texas Turnaround." I took the opportunity to add a subtitle to the *Business Facilities* article just below the picture of a beautiful Texas sunrise taken from Lookout Point, near Jacksonville. It read "Texas: You Ain't Seen Nothin' Yet!"

This change in attitude, particularly on the part of some of the reporters around the country, was amusing in some ways. Maybe I was closer to this whole phenomenon than most folks because I get called all the time by my friends from the media to provide economic data and offer my opinions on what's happening. Reporters who had sought me out throughout the year for background information on stories about Texas now phoned with a completely different tone. Even a month earlier, they had still persisted in writing stories or airing television news segments about the bad times in Texas, despite some clear signs that things were getting better. I sure tried to make that point over and over again, assuring anybody who asked that a significant recovery was indeed underway. I faxed numbers, drew pictures, told anecdotes, and screamed bloody murder about how well we were doing. After all, this upswing had been going on for more than a year, and it was high time that somebody knew about it.

I told as many stories as possible to illustrate the comeback in Texas. I talked about the company that used to make pipe for oil wells that was now making golf course irrigation systems. I related the true tale of the gasoline distributor who was now marketing a software system to track customer consumption at high-tech stations that operated without attendants. I spewed forth about all of the innovative programs that were underway in Beaumont, and the marvelous results they were getting. I had recently participated in their second Economic Summit, which was attended by thousands of local citizens. It was the nation's largest economic development rally. Whatever I said, I just couldn't seem to counteract the prevailing attitude that things were generally still bad.

Then, the scales suddenly fell from everyone's eyes. After the Super Collider, Fujitsu, GTE, my speech in Midland, Formosa Plastics, and all that stuff, the very same reporters who had been bashing us were starting to write and film stories about the "Great Texas Turnaround." They would call and ask me questions that were identical to the ones they'd just been asking a few weeks earlier, but now they were listening. They began to accept the real answers.

Even though the economic fortunes of the state had not changed radically in any real sense during those three or four weeks, perceptions had changed dramatically. Information about the future, such as corporate relocations and new research facilities, caused people to start looking at the present, instead of dwelling on the past. That in and of itself seemed like a healthy sign to me. Perceptions were turning positive, and this time they were pretty much mirroring reality. Ray's Law of Economics was working in the right direction. When people think we're on the mend, it makes it a whole lot easier to pull together all the ingredients (especially money) that it takes to make big things come to pass. After that, it was a whole lot easier to get deals saucered and blowed. (That phrase derives from a lot of the old folks over in East Texas, including my Pop. They didn't drink their morning coffee from the cup. They would pour it in the saucer, blow on it, and then take it down. When something has already been saucered and blowed, it's pretty much going to happen.)

My funniest experience during this time revolved around the Fujitsu announcement. This key facility was to be located on property owned by The Perot Group, the real estate arm of the Perot family interests, and translated into thousands of new jobs for the Dallas/Fort Worth area. I was working closely on this and other projects with The Perot Group, preparing economic impact studies, fiscal assessments for the affected communities, feasibility analyses, and other relevant statistics. The Fujitsu deal was all supposed to be very hush-hush until the news officially broke. As is always the case in matters of this nature, we were sworn to secrecy until the absolute last minute. On the day before the planned announcement, everybody in my office was scrambling to pull together the final numbers to be used in presentations, handouts, and the governor's speech. As usual, all rolled out smoothly the following morning, as though we had been messing with it for years.

It just so happened that one of the television networks had a crew from New York in my office in Waco that day taping their version of the "Great Texas Turnaround." (When folks from New York come to Waco, you know they're serious. On occasion I've even managed to lure cameras and lights from Tokyo to Waco.) At the request of the sound engineer, we dutifully tied up the phones and made all the other arrangements to have an appropriate degree of silence while the reporter did the interview and the cameras rolled. Our fax machine in the back was still on, however, and we kept getting urgent faxed messages, sometimes in pretty graphic language, telling us that our phones were inaccessible.

Once the interview was finally over and we flipped the switch, our phone lines looked like the flashing lights of a Christmas display in Neiman-Marcus's window. We then had the difficult task of offering cordial farewells to a very competent television news crew who obviously was aware that something was in the works. We had to gently shoo them out the door, while maintaining the secrecy that was so vital to this process. Our new receptionist, Jan Rowell (who now runs the Waco side of my life), was valiantly trying not to mention specific names of the callers on the other end of the phones until we had our media friends safely packed away. Somehow we got them out of there before they started asking too many embarrassing questions. Boy, did they miss a scoop! Sighs of relief could be heard for miles as the last one went out the door. That was one of the more frantic afternoons of my life, but for the privilege of being involved in an initiative that would bring several thousand new high-tech jobs to Texas, I would gladly take that kind of excitement any day. In fact, I'd be less than honest if I didn't confess that I love it.

During 1988, in addition to being in the midst of a number of economic development and relocation projects, I had my first (but, unfortunately, not my last) taste of the arena of lender liability. I was a witness for one of the former Allied Banks regarding some property, north of Austin, on which they held notes. They were being sued for not lending a developer the money to build some infrastructure (lights, streets, water lines, etc.) in a proposed industrial park, also known as a cow pasture. It didn't seem to matter that there was already enough fancy developed land in that area to last well into the next century. Lender liability litigation related to real estate has become a major growth industry in Texas and elsewhere as the banking and thrift situation has worsened. It seems that some of the folks who used to speculate on property are finding that, in today's environment, it might well be more fruitful to speculate on the judicial system.

By 1989, we were definitely out of the woods, but it was still no picnic. There were even more signs of vitality, and they were showing up in every sector. It was the third year of expansion. For example, by now, the state had more jobs than it had ever had before—even at the height of the boom. Whole subdivisions of houses in Houston which had been vacant and which nobody could sell were suddenly being snapped up, and no longer at fire-sale prices. These were just a few of the signs. There were many more.

As I said, though, it wasn't a picnic; at least not one without a lot of Texas fire ants. During the final year of this turbulent decade, there were still more real estate companies and banks that had to seek shelter within the confines of federal bankruptcy laws and deposit insurance funds. Among the prominent Texas casualties that year were Southmark and Lomas. My office has been involved in working with both of these organizations, in helping to value their real estate holdings, restructure their portfolios, and perform other tasks to assist in realistic reorganizations. In the process of this work, I have become more and more optimistic and am now convinced that viable plans can be achieved which permit an opportunity to obtain reasonable value from the remaining assets.

From a publicity standpoint, Texas has obviously taken its lumps, newswise, about all the difficulties that hit major companies and financial institutions. Nevertheless, the overall attitude has shifted to the point that the good news outweighs the bad. The world's perception is now undeniably centered on the fact that the state is in the midst of a major business expansion and that investment opportunities abound.

My first major episode of 1989 was in helping to secure passage of the referendum to build a domed stadium in San Antonio. We first performed a feasibility study to see if it made sense and, boy, did it ever. The Alamo City has a multibillion dollar tourism industry that pulls in major conventions every week. Just think what it can do with a first-class facility. In early January, the initiative was behind in the polls and faced stern opposition on several fronts. I made speeches, conducted press conferences and briefings, debated, did live interviews, prepared summaries, drew pictures, and whatever else I thought might help. In mid-January, the voters approved the "Alamodome" proposal by a comfortable margin. A lot of local business leaders and other civic-minded individuals worked night and day to pull this one off, and I was glad that I could help.

The real hero of that particular Battle of the Alamo, however, was none other than "His Honor," then San Antonio Mayor Henry Cisneros. By that point, Henry's personal life was making headlines, and he decided not to seek another term. He threw himself into this project like a man possessed. He stumped, debated, cajoled, negotiated, and did all of the things that a gifted public warrior does for a cause that he believes in. He showed a lot of grit under difficult circumstances, and I was glad to be a small part of his winning team. I hope that Texas gets the benefit of his unique leadership capacity in the future (although I wish he wasn't quite so tall). Later in the year, I had an opportunity to be involved in a similar successful endeavor to fund a more modest convention facility in Austin. It's exciting to witness the birth of new economic generators.

On a less pleasant, but nonetheless productive, front, Congress was finally beginning to face up to the realities of the financial crisis to a greater extent, passing new legislation which put some money into the process and created the Resolution Trust Corporation. This is a governmental institution that is supposed to warehouse all of the assets of the failed financial institutions and sell them off in an orderly fashion. With the passage of the RTC bill, the federal government became the largest landowner in Texas—indeed, the world's largest property management operation. It is already apparent that additional funds will be required to bring the "cleanup" process to final fruition. Our elected officials simply can't swallow $500 billion in one lump. (By the way, if you write it out, it looks like this: $500,000,000,000.00. It's really an awesome number.)

Interestingly, when some overall statistics were compiled on the subject, it was found that, despite all the outcry from Washington about "S&L crooks" (and there were certainly some Texas culprits among them), the shady dealers account for only $5 billion of the overall losses. If that number is close to accurate, it is only roughly 1% of what I expect the total cost to be. So really, when you get right down to it, very little of this problem is due to outright fraud, despite a lot of emotionally-charged coverage of the "bad guys." Most of the losses actually came from the factors that I have talked about in these pages, and the effects they had on what people thought. Changing tax codes, financial deregulation, greed, stupidity, and unfulfilled expectations all had a role to play in the process. The forces were so powerful that, in a highly publicized project that we released in 1987, we discovered and became the first to say that the excessive lending was so rampant that it actually became a cause, rather than a by-product, of some of the economic malaise. As I said earlier, the situation that produced this disaster was as rare as the mutual alignment of nine planets.

1989 was the time, however, when the national magnitude of this crisis was realized, and initial steps toward a long-term solution were taken. Texas had already lived through the worst of it, and much of the remaining drama would be played out on stages with other names, like New England, California, and the South Atlantic Coast.

The general attitude around the world at the present time is that Texas now represents an excellent investment opportunity. I found that to be true in my travels during '89 and still do. The final year of the 1980s contributed to this newly-positive perception with still more rounds of very upbeat corporate relocation announcements, and some turning around of earnings reports on the part of well-known Texas entities. Fruit of the Loom announced a major facility in Harlingen. There were also major relocations announced by MCI, Exxon, and several petrochemical firms. Many other companies, such as Motorola, Texas Instruments, and Tandy, continued to expand their Texas operations.

On the state legislative front, Texas finally took the bull by the horns on tort reform. One of the most intriguing issues facing the 1989 regular session surrounded the civil justice system of Texas. The overall justice system, particularly workers' compensation rates and guidelines, had long been viewed as a primary detriment to the business climate of Texas. As I've said, Texas law has an extremely Populist tradition. It comes out in our attitudes regarding taxes, banking, utilities, and just about every other institution within the state. To top it off, our laws have been interpreted by elected appellate judges, many of whom receive large campaign contributions from the plaintiffs' attorneys who represent the Populist point of view. There has to be some balance in civil law between the interests of the individual and the interests of business, but we have a reputation for a system that skews that precarious pendulum too much in one direction. This perception has scared off some investment dollars and discouraged many "home grown" Texas companies from expanding within the state.

Many other aspects of the Texas business climate had already been improved by legislation over the past few years. Enterprise zones, specific incentive programs, promotional campaigns, foreign offices, and countless other initiatives had passed from the drawing board to the legislative floor to the governor's desk to reality. Of lingering concern to many people, however, was the civil justice system. Our workers' compensation, product liability, and deceptive trade practice laws were a cause of great concern for businesses in Texas and certainly for those who were thinking about locating here. Our insurance rates were much higher than those of many other states, and fears of Texas courts were rampant. When weighted on a per-worker basis, we ranked among the top ten states in the country in premiums paid and among the bottom ten in benefits received. Although it wasn't related to a personal injury or a product liability issue, the multibillion dollar verdict in the Pennzoil-Texaco case caused a flood of negative publicity about the judicial process in Texas. (The fact that the case was won by a legal team led by Joe Jamail, one of the preeminent trial lawyers in the country, was obviously a contributing factor.)

One study that we did as part of the legislative process indicated that the losses from product liability alone in terms of jobs in Texas exceeded those gained from all of the direct, indirect, and induced effects of Sematech, the Super Collider, Formosa Plastics, GTE, and Fujitsu combined. Workers' compensation, however, was the top priority and became House Bill #1. Although the legislative session opened with much fanfare about this initiative, intense lobbying persisted through several special sessions before a modest reform measure was finally enacted as the passage from the 1980s to the 1990s was occurring. We still have a long way to go on this one, but the momentum is shifting. Like so many other things in our decade of disintegration, it ultimately came down to the lifeblood of all economies—jobs.

Some other factors are also tempering the judicial climate as the new decade begins. For one, the voters changed the composition of the Texas Supreme Court considerably. They, too, got the message that thousands of current and potential future jobs were at stake. For another, two major, highly publicized civil trials occurred in which juries in Houston brought forth verdicts for the defense. One was a case against Monsanto Corporation related to a subdivision located near the old Brio refinery site in the southern part of Houston. The other suit was an anti-trust action brought against *The Dallas Morning News* by the rival *Dallas Times Herald* over the rights to publish "Geech," "Doonesbury," and a few other features. I was privileged to be a part of the defense team in both instances. Hopefully, these jury findings will ease some of the unfortunate and undeserved stigma attached to Houston courts in the aftermath of Pennzoil-Texaco. Folks on the Gulf Coast can weigh the evidence and render reasonable opinions as well as anyone else.

For many people in Texas, and certainly for me, by far the most exciting announcement of the year was the decision by American Airlines to put its new aircraft maintenance facility at Fort Worth Alliance Airport. The potential for this innovative industrial hub is tremendous. I have had the privilege of being involved in many initiatives over the past seven or eight years. I've cut more than a few ribbons, put a lot of gold shovels in the ground, and been a part of more projects than I can count. I rode around in a four-wheeler over the bumpy terrain of the future Homeport site near Corpus Christi long before any machinery was moved in to level the ground.

I've seen them all, but Alliance is really something special. At a location where Interstate-35 West and the Santa Fe Railroad run very close together, a new airport was conceived and designed exclusively for industrial use. It permits raw materials and components to be brought in by rail, truck, or plane. Assembly of any product can take place at Alliance with distribution again being possible through the very best of all three key transportation modes. It is truly a glimpse into the future of the international production complex. I was involved both in the original impact studies for the American Airlines maintenance base and the site selection work for the company that resulted in the final choice. I have also worked with other firms that will soon call Alliance their home.

One of the hardest things I have to do in this part of my work, but something which professional responsibility and integrity requires, is to provide unbiased and objective analysis of alternative sites around the country. It killed me to have to do this with the American maintenance base proposal, but I dutifully drew up a thorough analysis of a site in Oklahoma City (which, I might add, was an outstanding candidate in its own right). But Texas won out.

The exciting thing to me about American's decision was simply the fact that it was made before the airport was even finished. The investment of hundreds of millions of dollars at this early stage was certainly a strong testimonial to the viability of this concept. Through the vision and persistence of former Speaker of the House Jim Wright, Mayor Bob Bolen of Fort Worth, H. Ross Perot, and Ross Perot, Jr., the Alliance facility became a reality in a remarkably short period of time. The Federal Aviation Administration (FAA) had originally envisioned a smaller general aviation facility to be opened around the turn of the century. Through an aggressive public-private cooperative endeavor, however, it became the nation's only full-service industrial airport much sooner. One of the private goals of the participants was to land a plane in the 1980s. Sure enough, just before Christmas in 1989, the runway was ready to go.

The Alliance complex defines the way that manufacturing and distribution will take place in the next century. It is also strategically located in a geographic area that is perfect for a transportation hub, but one that has not yet seen substantial economic development. In fact, the region is the principal remaining corridor in the Dallas/Fort Worth Metroplex that is not intensely settled. With its general proximity to the Treasury Department's currency plant, the Motorola facilities, IBM's operations, and DFW Airport, it represents one of the most ideal locations that could possibly be found. The communities around Alliance are also going through a careful planning program to assure that growth is achieved in a productive and positive manner that also maintains a high quality of life for those who live and work there.

Alliance Airport and American's maintenance base managed to bring tears to my eyes on three separate occasions during 1989, which is a tough thing for a kid from East Texas to admit. The first was on the day in June that American officially announced its decision. We knew that all of our hundreds of hours of hard work were coming to fruition and that the concept that was Alliance Airport was being validated. As Bob Crandall, American's Chief Executive Officer, made the formal proclamation in a crowded Fort Worth City Hall, I was completely overcome with emotion. Thousands of good jobs and hundreds of millions of dollars were coming to Texas, and it felt absolutely great.

One critical aspect of this decision on the part of American was that Texas had effectively responded to an unprecedented incentive package put together by the State of Oklahoma. Pulling this one off took a tremendous amount of legislative maneuvering in a very tight time frame. The whole deal almost came unraveled during the summer and fall, however, as the tax abatements that were a part of the deal met with considerable resistance at Northwest Independent School District. The ensuing negotiations were a very legitimate and normal process in which everyone was seeking the best interests of the local students. There were short-term and long-term considerations, and a vision of the future that was very difficult to see from the vantage point of the present. The final vote was taken by the school board in late September in a crowded auditorium at the local high school after several hours of debate. It seemed like it had been weeks since any of us had slept. The vote was unanimous. The abatements were approved. The deal was saucered and blowed. Bulldozers started moving dirt on the maintenance base the very next morning, and I was again overcome with emotion.

The third time it hit me came on a very cold and windy day as the year was drawing to a close. I was standing on the runway at Alliance. In a dramatic ceremony, an American Airlines jet passed by and then landed smoothly on its new concrete carpet. The door opened, and Santa Claus became the first passenger to disembark. As he waved to the crowd—young and old alike, prominent and unknown, rich and poor—I couldn't help but think of the promise that this facility held for the future of Texas. It was December of 1989, and it felt good.

My million miles of travel in a single decade were almost behind me. Like all of Texas, I could look forward to the future with tremendous enthusiasm and renewed optimism. Alliance was a reality, and all sorts of other business initiatives were pushing forward. Basically, although it hadn't been all uphill, Texas as a whole was in a third year of economic recovery and about to enter a fourth. In just a few days and a few miles away from this new runway, I would find myself at that New Year's Eve party that I talked about in the very beginning. It had indeed been quite a decade. We'd been rode hard and put up wet. But we were able to get the kinks out and were off and running again. At that moment, it hit me. We had, indeed, survived.

TEN

. . . And Conquer

Well, we made it. The '80s are behind us now. As unequivocal evidence of this fact, Billy Bob's Texas, the humongous club at the Fort Worth Stockyards, opened with great fanfare during the oil boom, closed in financial disarray during the bust, and now once again is alive and flourishing. We have been in a recovery since late 1987 and, while I know there will be ups and downs, I have publicly projected that the state's growth will exceed that of the nation over the next two decades. I'm out on a limb, as usual. Although the pace of the oil boom is not likely to return any time soon, we are entering a new era of prosperity. To borrow and slightly fracture a quote from President Bush, we are embarking on a "kinder, gentler" period for the Texas economy.

There were plenty of times during the crazy swings of our last ten years that we all wondered whether we were going to make it at all. With the aid of the indomitable spirit of Texas, a lot of hard work, and a good dose of luck, we prevailed. That's not to say that we arrived at the end of the 1980s basking in the same glory that we enjoyed as we entered the decade. We have scars that will be with us for a while. We have not yet resolved all of the real estate and financial problems, and won't for quite some time. We're sure to see a few more headlines on that one.

The fact that peace seemed to be "breaking out" all over the world as the 1990s began has also caused concern for some Texans (although tensions erupting in the Middle East as this book is going to press may change all of that). While it is hard to be against a world filled with international harmony and tranquility, there is little doubt that Texas has a significant presence of military bases, hospitals, defense contracts, and other linkages to the maintenance of a large and highly sophisticated military presence around the globe. Cutbacks in federal spending and changes in priorities may cause some disruptions and dislocations in impacted areas, particularly over the next few years. At the same time, the oil markets are anything but settled, and the state is facing enormous challenges with regard to its educational and social service systems. In short, we still have a lot of stuff left to do.

With all of these things staring us in the face, why do I project that Texas will be on an upward track? Why will we "conquer" in the 1990s? There are several reasons. For one thing, we began the 1990s on a very positive note. Despite all of the ups and downs of the 1980s, the past two and a half years have clearly emerged on the plus side of the ledger. We ended the decade with about 6.9 million non-agricultural jobs; we began with about 5.7 million workers. When you look at them year by year, the numbers that comprise that gain do not begin to compare in absolute or percentage terms to the leaps of steady upward growth enjoyed during the "oil boom." Nonetheless, they illustrate that, although we had dramatic highs and lows, gaining and losing equivalents of the entire work force of Alaska with reckless abandon, we came out on top. Over a million jobs (about six Alaskas) is nothing to sneeze at, no matter how high the ragweed count gets in Central Texas. The real gross state product, or total production in Texas, ended up at about $310 billion, higher than it has ever been and a full 30% above the level that we recorded as the decade began. Not bad for a bunch of goat ropers and cowchip throwers who had their legs chopped off at the knees twice in the same decade.

Second, we genuinely achieved an important measure of diversification during the 1980s. For much of the decade, I felt a little like a preacher as I stumped the state extolling the virtues of economic development and a more balanced industrial mix. At first, nobody really listened. We had made a pretty big deal out of new facilities in the heyday of the old Texas Industrial Commission (the late 1950s and 1960s). During the oil boom, however, we hardly even talked about it. It just sort of came natural, like dancing when you hear a Bob Wills song. As the '80s were cranking up and petroleum prices faltered, there were a few folks trying their best, but it was hard to build a constituency.

One of the unsung heroes of this time was Harden Wiedemann, a young Dallasite who put in a noteworthy stint running the Texas Economic Development Commission (a descendent of the Texas Industrial Commission, which was later absorbed into the Texas Department of Commerce). Harden did a great job with limited resources and support, and continues to work on new initiatives in the private sector to keep Texas rolling down the right path. Nowadays, everybody takes the whole process a lot more seriously.

Although the task of broadening our economic base is evolutionary and ongoing, Texas has clearly made remarkable strides since the beginning of the 1980s. We're getting there. Our dependence on the oil and gas sector has declined. As I said, we have over a million more workers now than we had at the beginning of that fateful decade. Nevertheless, we've been net losers of jobs in our former bellwether sectors, including mineral extraction and manufacturing facilities tied directly to oil and gas drilling activity. You only have to drive by one or two fields of plugged wells, or see a few of those old seesaw-looking pumps standing idle, to know that things ain't what they used to be. A quick pass through the once vibrant industrial park in Alice will also do the trick.

On the other hand, we have seen a lot of increases in the production of high tech equipment (such as electronics and telecommunications apparatus), air transportation, health care, and aircraft manufacturing. In so doing, we have established a notable presence in the growth industries of the future. It's really very simple. We have a lot more jobs, and fewer of them are tied to natural resources. We're meeting the challenge.

Broad-based diversification is really the key to our staying power over the long haul. I've been a strong proponent of this agenda for quite a while, even well before "The Speech" in 1984. The whole point of that address was that it was not enough just to talk about and recruit "high tech" firms. We had to look at all the horseshoes and try to wear as many as would fit.

I certainly don't think it was my speech at the Lyceum that did the trick, although maybe it helped a little. My efforts around the state in that direction have had some effect. I read somewhere that I was involved in projects that brought over 100,000 jobs to the Lone Star State in a single year. That may be true; I never stop to count. On a day-to-day basis, however, it's the sweat and toil of thousands of community leaders down in the trenches throughout Texas that make things happen. I do think that we were able to foster widespread acceptance of the concept that information, hard work, and patience can pay off in positive economic outcomes. It seems that a lot of people in Texas in positions to do something about it got the message. Because of a whole bunch of development efforts in many different parts of the state, a lot of jobs have been created and a bunch of exciting new programs are in place. All such efforts, big and small, are important to our overall growth. I didn't care whether we're talking about 5 jobs or 5,000 jobs. At the end of the 1980s, we were well underway in the process of building a more diversified economic base.

Another thing that happened is that once we were bitten by the economic development bug, we got a lot smarter and more aggressive. (Earlier, we had treated this "bug" like a big Texas mosquito; we didn't want to be anywhere around it.) We learned that you have to go out and make the opportunities. We found out that regional cooperation, even among cities that are major rivals, often works to the benefit of everyone. We learned about prospecting, incentives, infrastructure, and a lot of other things that were given very little attention during the 1970s. We became familiar with the value of foreign trade zones, enterprise zones, and the capacity to cut through red tape. We established government contract centers, small business development centers, incubators, and other avenues to attract new investment. We created programs to focus exclusively on business retention. Helping small businesses and keeping existing companies viable can often do as much for an area as a highly publicized relocation. Major new facilities that create thousands of jobs are exciting and fun. They can always be counted on to garner the headlines, as well they should. In the final analysis, though, we figured out that the progress of economies often takes place quietly. A lot more of it comes one or two jobs at a time than any other way. We recognized the need for a broad-based constituency in business development, and we did something about it.

You have to understand that many of these efforts are very un-Texan things, or at least things that Texans didn't do in the past. In the good old days, the most common strategy on the part of many chambers of commerce was to go to work in the morning, raise the flag, and focus on local issues until that fateful day when the electric utility or the railroad brought in a prospect. At that point, everyone shifted into gear. They gave out the brochure they had printed up four or five years ago, showed off vacant buildings and raw tracts of land as if they were pure gold, and made sure their visitor understood that what made their city really special was the quality of life. (How many times have I heard that last one?) It was definitely a reactive rather than a proactive response. We waited for folks to come to us; we didn't go out and grab 'em by the collar. Once the prospect left, it was back to business as usual.

In the 1980s, however, several factors combined to change the mode of operation. First, the sheer number of new plants out there somewhere that we might want to recruit was on the decline. Second, as industry became more technologically-oriented and the United States moved toward a service-based economy, the focus changed. All of a sudden, some major employers cropped up that didn't have any great need to be large consumers of electricity. The role of the railroads in the process had declined years earlier. For many of the new growth industries, telecommunications infrastructure is far more important than the more traditional resource requirements. The only things they need from the power folks are lights and a few regular old plugs to make their computers sing.

At the same time, some of the utilities within the state found themselves facing budgetary constraints. They had built the capacity to serve a booming economy, and the boom was lowered. Increased cost and revenues that were below expectations put a serious crimp in their ability to be as aggressive as they had been in more prosperous times. The electric companies remain a valuable part of the process, but a different environment has brought new challenges that have to be met by a broader constituency. It just takes more folks to get the job done. Texas is responding to that challenge.

The 1980s also taught us the importance of competing in the international arena and of providing the types of incentives that were needed for major locations. Increasingly, labor intensive companies are leaving Texas to take advantage of cheaper workers in other countries. On the other hand, plants, money, joint ventures, and other activities are increasingly bringing foreign investors to

Texas. At the beginning of the decade, we had no active foreign development initiatives, with the exception of a modest effort in Mexico. Now, we're doing pretty well. The state has programs, a number of cities have initiatives, and a lot of consultants and developers are actively involved. We've also come up with ways to get a slice of the huge pie that is baked by filling supply orders for the low-wage assembly plants in other lands. I recently participated in the Economic Summit of Industrialized Nations in Houston. The leaders of the major powers of the free world gathered to talk about a radical new business and trade environment. Unlike days gone by, Texans kept a very watchful eye on this event. Things really have changed a lot. I now go over to small towns in East Texas and have people bombard me with questions about how they can get involved internationally. Ten years ago, they didn't want people coming in from Oklahoma, much less Korea.

With regard to incentives, we had a hard time figuring out the rules. At first, everybody was against it. Period. If folks wanted the privilege of coming to Texas, they could do it on our terms. Then a bunch of towns jumped on the bandwagon and went absolutely crazy. They would give away the store and get very little in return. The secret is to strike a balance. Provide the incentives that are needed. Make the deals happen. Understand the requirements of a given situation. Create a "win-win" scenario for the company and the community. That's how the process works. We began to appreciate that concept during the course of the 1980s.

The decision by Sematech to come to Austin is a classic example of the right way to do it. Numerous cities throughout the country offered proposals to this prestigious manufacturing and research consortium. Many of them contained a much higher dollar value than the deal that was put together by Austin; at least one was more than four times as large. Nonetheless, Austin was systematic in providing precisely the resources that were needed. That's the ticket. We have to be a little smarter than the other folks. Increasingly throughout the decade, cities, chambers of commerce, industrial foundations, counties, regional planning agencies, and others learned the value of having full-time professional personnel with experience in industrial development running their activities. There was a time when it seemed like the only two growth occupations in Texas were arsonists and economic development specialists.

Perhaps the most important lesson we learned throughout the decade was that information was the single most essential (and underestimated) resource in economic development efforts. It was this simple realization that brought me and my colleagues into this arena at the outset. People began to ring me up and say that they knew they wanted to do something, that they were committed to development, but that they didn't even know what they had to promote. They didn't have a clue as to where to start. In communities throughout Texas, we were able to supply them with a jumping-off point for their efforts. We could find the information, analyze it, put it in a usable form, and make recommendations based on it. As our data base, contact base, and resource base grew throughout the decade, we found ourselves repeatedly in a position to refine the process even more. We were able to match specific prospects with specific community assets and to respond quickly and effectively with relevant materials. This capacity helped Texas cities to be a lot more competitive in the site selection process.

In short, the Texas economy is in a much better position today to sustain long-term diversified expansion than it was a decade ago. If I could walk into a laboratory and design my own model economy, and I had my choice of starting with the one that existed in Texas on January 1, 1980 or the one that existed on January 1, 1990, I would pick the new one without any hesitation whatsoever. At first glance, that statement may seem ludicrous. After all, 1980 was a euphoric high for Texas, with soaring oil prices, and a booming economy. We were the envy of the entire world. In comparison, the situation as we start the 1990s may seem a bit meager. If you stop and think about it, though, the Texas economy is not nearly as vulnerable to fluctuations in the price of a single commodity that trades in a highly erratic market environment as it was ten years ago. One of the most positive signs about the current recovery is that, since it began around mid-1987, the price of oil has made a couple of trips up and down the ladder, but the economy hasn't. Through it all, we've been able to keep on climbing.

That is not to say that Texas has declared independence from the dominion of oil or that its price is not important to our prospects. Oil remains a significant natural resource endowment, and its price will remain a critical factor in determining the path of our state for many years to come. As this book was going to press, Iraq invaded Kuwait. Immediately, oil prices started climbing. If these increases stick for awhile, Texas will do better than it would have otherwise. The future of petroleum and the future of Texas are inextricably linked. Oil will indeed be vital, but it won't be the only factor. We have not begun to exhaust all of the reserves within the state, although we have extracted quite a bit of the part that can be obtained through relatively straightforward and inexpensive technologies.

The secret to diversification is not total independence from oil, but having oil as well as other things. We can't afford to be totally subject to the whims of folks in the Middle East. We've been down that road before. One of the first things we tell the communities that we work with throughout the country is to "build from strength." In the case of Texas, oil is definitely a strength. It is a non-renewable natural resource that is used everyday by just about everybody in the world. The whole point of diversification, in fact, the very definition of the word, is not to put all of your eggs in one basket. We need to have a mix of industries, some that benefit from lower petroleum prices and others that prosper from higher prices. For good measure, we might want to throw in a few that really don't care much one way or the other. When you get to that point, even though some industries lose, others profit when the oil markets fluctuate in either direction. It is a balancing act that keeps the overall economy on a more even keel. Texas is clearly not all the way there yet, but we're a lot closer now than we were ten years ago.

By far the most compelling reason for a bright outlook for the future is much more fundamental than anything that I've mentioned so far. The simple truth is that the long-term prospects for any area are driven by three fundamental factors: natural resources, technology, and human resources. And in Texas, despite our recessionary difficulties in the recent past, all three remain strong.

I remember as I traveled around the state and elsewhere in the depths of the 1986 recession, I would project that Texas would grow more rapidly than the nation over the next quarter-century. At the time, I'm afraid that people often thought I was more than a little bit crazy (of course, that wasn't the first time, nor the last). The notion that we actually had a strong underlying base for future expansion was considered farfetched by many of my colleagues, the press, and a lot of the folks who heard me talk about it. They just couldn't see past the daily devastation of the oil price collapse. Now that they realize that we made it through that mess with all of our fingers and toes intact, more and more of them are coming around to my way of thinking.

The funny thing about that whole episode is the way short-term distractions can at times cloud the long-term judgment of even the most experienced and acute observers. Things like expected patterns in natural resources and the demographic characteristics of the population rarely change all that much in a short span of time, certainly not in four years. Their general patterns in 1990 are not radically different than they were in 1986. You can just see a little farther out when it's not so foggy all around you.

When folks like myself venture into short-term forecasting, we worry about short-term matters. We look closely at such things as the mood at the Federal Reserve, any pending tax or regulatory changes, the collective blood pressure of the oil ministers, and any one of countless other phenomena that may be relevant at a given point in time. Folks sometimes get all excited about some pretty silly things, and we try to keep an eye on all of them. We have to. Those things are all important trail signs for someone who tracks the path of the economy for a few months or quarters into the future.

Over the long haul, however, many of these factors tend to cancel one another. We get to look at stuff that is a lot more important (and interesting) than an oil minister with an ingrown toenail or a politician having an affair. In terms of more traditional indicators, oil prices and interest rates tend to be up at times and down at times. It pretty well averages out over twenty years or so. When we put together a long-term forecast, we have a chance to get out of the trees and look at the forest. And for Texas, right now, the long view looks just fine. (Longview's not doing too badly, either.) All of the phenomena that define long-term potential are showing positive fundamentals. With regard to natural resources, it is obvious that Texas enjoys advantages over most other places on this planet or any other. We've always had rich endowments of oil, natural gas, and lignite, as well as great expanses of timber. That natural bounty is not going away any time soon. We also have other mineral resources, fertile agricultural land, and, in many areas of the state, adequate water supplies that, with prudent conservation and planning, will support business expansion for an extended period of time.

In the realm of technology, the state also seems poised to be very competitive in the future. Although the state and, indeed, the entire country have lagged in the race to the twenty-first century at times in the recent past, there is little doubt that Texas is emerging as a major center for the creation and implementation of new technologies. All of that talk about "high tech," and the action that it spurred, helped us to make some significant strides. The IBM robotics center in the Metroplex, MCC and Sematech in Austin, the biomedical complex being created by the Houston Area Research Council, the Texas Research Park in San Antonio, and numerous other initiatives are a good start and bode well for future growth in this whole area. The Super Collider promises to bring Texas its first major national research laboratory and, with it, millions of federal dollars each year.

The medical communities in Dallas, Houston, and San Antonio are poised for many new initiatives in technology creation and transfer. University-based research within the state is on the rise and the capacity to evolve pure research into commercial applications and take them to the marketplace is improving. Venture capital networks and clubs are aiding in the provision of investment capital for new ideas. Programs such as the "Texas First" initiative on the part of Southwestern Bell—a program in which the company will make huge capital investments in new equipment to upgrade rural service and provide virtually all of Texas with state-of-the-art facilities—should assure adequate telecommunications resources to support economic development throughout the state. With a fax machine and a phone and a computer tied to digitally-switched lines, you can do business just about anywhere.

The new Fujitsu facility in Richardson is one among several that will position Texas among the leaders in telecommunications research. There are also major firms in the state that are responsible for many new developments in space technology. The expansion of Compaq Computer in the Houston area continues at a fast clip. Throughout the world, the rate of technological implementation is increasing in exponential leaps, and Texas firms are likely to adapt in a competitive manner. In short, Texas should not be at a disadvantage in the technological race over the next few decades.

The final long-term resource is people, or, more accurately, workers. When you combine the natural resource base of an area with its work force and add in the capacity to make that work force more productive through new technologies, you pretty well define its potential growth path. There's just not much else to it. The daily headlines over the next few years will tell us many things about the world economy: developments in the Eastern

Bloc and the Persian Gulf, new trade relationships, policy changes, financial restructuring, and who knows what else may crop up. Who would ever have dreamed even a few years ago that, as the 1990s began, the Berlin Wall would tumble and we'd be looking at the phenomenon of a reunited Germany. We also wouldn't have thought that the bastions of Communism would begin to topple right and left, although more to the right than to the left.

You only have to think back to the 1960s to realize the folly of trying to guess all of the structural changes that will occur over an extended period of time. Had anyone seriously projected in, say, the mid-1960s that we would see a 20% prime rate of interest, $35 per barrel oil prices, a $200 billion federal deficit, the Third World debt crisis, or any one of a thousand other events, he or she would have been regarded as totally out of touch with anything approaching economic reality.

Whatever the headlines may turn out to be down the road, there is little doubt that one of the major underlying themes in our future is going to be a critical shortage of new workers. The reasons lie in simple demographics, and they were basically the same in 1986 as they are today. The "Baby Boom" that occurred in this country between 1945 and 1964 provided us with a steady supply of new workers over an extended period of time in the 1960s, '70s, and '80s. The number of people in the 20 to 24-year-old age group, however, peaked in 1982 at approximately 21.8 million. By the end of this decade the total will have fallen by more than 4.5 million folks. I'm not talking about a lower growth rate or any other mathematical hocus pocus; I'm talking about fewer bodies, pure and simple.

Bottlenecks in particular geographic regions and specific occupations are already surfacing. Much will be written and said about this phenomenon in the future. It is destined to put upward pressure on wage rates and encourage a still greater pace of technological innovation and attempts to substitute capital for labor. Another by-product is that those areas of the United States that have the capacity to provide new workers to a hungry marketplace will have an enormous competitive advantage in attracting new business activity. They really can't lose. The demographic patterns in Texas are quite conducive to meeting the labor needs of future production in this country. Texas will be among the leaders in the capacity to provide the single resource—entry level workers and a skilled labor force—that will be in greatest demand during the coming years. This simple fact virtually assures that the state will outpace the nation over an extended period of time.

Our competitive edge in this regard can be broadened considerably if Texas is successful in improving its educational infrastructure. Improvements should be made across the board, including everyone from the youngest members of the educational process to those in the upper echelons of the higher education system. We need help all the way from *Fun with Dick and Jane* to *Advanced Quantum Physics*. There is a particular need to focus on vocational and technical training of the finest quality to meet the labor demands created by new, evolving, and increasingly sophisticated industries. A large portion of the new positions that must be filled as the workplace of the next century takes shape will be in the types of occupations that require extensive technical skill. Expansion of programs at Texas State Technical Institute (our primary state-funded training system with campuses throughout Texas), the community colleges, the high schools, and private institutions is essential. We need to adopt an even broader perspective that embraces public-private partnerships, corporate training programs, and continuing education at the adult level to retrain workers and provide new skills. Activities of this nature can bring dramatic dividends to the state.

I repeat that the future of Texas is indeed bright. The economy is more than likely to experience cyclical fluctuations, some of which may occur over the next few years as the readjustments in defense policy come about. Over a more extended time horizon, however, the state may well have much more to gain from the opening of new export markets in Eastern Europe and elsewhere than it will lose in the short-term dislocations in the defense industry. Those prospects look quite good.

One of the obvious lessons to be learned from our experiences in the 1980s is simply that major dislocations in traditional resource-based industries and dramatic swings in business activity can indeed happen. There's perhaps an even more cogent lesson to be gleaned from our huge real estate and financial catastrophe. The overbuilding cycle came to Texas before it visited, and wreaked havoc on, other parts of the country. It happened here first because everybody had glowing perceptions about the boundless future prosperity in our state at the same time that new tax and financial regulations encouraging development came on the scene. We were victimized by Ray's Law of Economics. What people thought and, hence, planned for and invested in, turned out to be at serious odds with reality.

The broader focus of this lesson lies in the fact that the incentive system that started the frenzy remained essentially in place, with only minor modifications, until the new, stricter tax laws went into effect in 1987. Hence, as fortunes in Texas dampened, real estate folks and investors began looking for greener pastures elsewhere. They didn't dismantle the cranes; they just moved them. The same excessive development and the attendant raw land speculation that plagued Texas occurred in other parts of the country a few years later, and the cycle of seriously depressed values and calamity among lenders is now being repeated in various parts of the country. I recently received a call from a good friend and fellow economist in New England (I do have a precious few Yankee friends) who asked me, "How do you know when you're dead?"

Hopefully, what Texas went through will help in some way to minimize the disruptions in other parts of the country. Our experience should act as a guide to other regions. Those of us who cut our teeth on the workout process for the Lone Star State can constructively assist other areas as the nation pulls through this mind-boggling financial restructuring process. That is certainly not a role that Texas is accustomed to playing in the annals of history, but we do have a long-standing tradition of being willing to lend a helping hand to a neighbor in need. So, why not?

The 1980s are behind us now. We have lived through adversity and gone a long way toward coming out of it. From seemingly barren ground, new growth has sprung. I am still amazed at the role that I had the privilege of playing simply because I held the key to a storehouse of information. When I began the decade as a naive young academic, I had no idea that I would be in a position to be "at the party" so many times. It was certainly not the kind of party Texas expected to have at all. It was more like a fraternity bash that got out of hand than a celebration, and we're still sweeping up the debris.

When I began building my initial model for Texas in the early '80s, I anticipated I would spend plenty of time telling people in other parts of the country how lucky we were to be in Texas and how we wished they could be doing as well as we were. By the time I released my first forecast from that model, the walls of the cathedral were pretty shaky. As I began to travel around the state and see the enormous human suffering that accompanies economic dislocations, my modest initial interest in development quickly turned into a magnificent obsession and a mission that would drive me to work harder and faster to try to play a constructive role in turning things around. As we face the future, I look forward to even more challenges along these lines.

I think our primary long-term achievement is that we firmly established the premise in Texas in the 1980s that information could be effectively used to achieve strategic economic advantages. It is a key economic resource that can (and should) even be viewed as part of the infrastructure required to support a competitive business environment. The same dictum can be applied on a national and international basis, and I hope to be a part of that process in other parts of the world as well. While my efforts were almost totally focused on Texas during most of the '80s, like Texas itself, we are rapidly expanding our universe in the 1990s. Of course, my first love and priority will always be for the state that I have called home since the day that I was born (December 25, 1952).

Global forces shaped the economy of Texas in the 1980s, and there is little that any individual human endeavor could have done to prevent the wild swings that occurred. They are much easier to explain than they were to endure. Nevertheless, the state has responded in many positive ways and positioned itself for a more stable and diversified economic future. We have a lot to look forward to in a dynamic international environment that will, inevitably, undergo still more radical and unforeseen changes. For now, suffice it to say that we have, indeed, survived. In fact, there's every reason to believe that we're now ready to go out and conquer.

As the '80s were winding down, Kenny Rogers recorded a surrealistic song about "the biggest place in outer space, the Planet Texas." Who knows? We just might make it! The eyes of Texas, after a bleary decade, are clearly and squarely focused on the world and, indeed, the universe. As I said earlier, "You ain't seen nothin' yet!"